Responsive Readings
for the
Modern Church

A study in the relationship between Bible
scriptures in a responsive reading format for use
in corporate worship or personal study.

Published by eBookIt.com
http://www.eBookIt.com

ISBN-13: 978-1-4566-2673-0 (Amazon KDP)
ISBN-13: 978-1-4566-3714-9 (Paperback)

David Rhodes is a retired missionary who served from 1999 through 2008 with Kids Alive International at the Lima Children's Home in Lima, Peru in the capacity of Maintenance and Construction Supervisor. He also served from 2009 through 2017 with SonSet Solutions at their facility in Elkhart, Indiana in the capacity of Operations Manager and Projects Coordinator.

Table of Contents

ONE

A selection of scriptural readings based on word subjects

Hebrews 4:12 New International Version (NIV)

For the word of God is alive and active. Sharper than any double-edged sword, it penetrates even to dividing soul and spirit, joints and marrow; it judges the thoughts and attitudes of the heart.

Angel

Was not our father Abraham considered righteous for what he did when he offered his son Isaac on the alter?[1]

But the *angel* of the Lord called out to him from heaven, "Abraham! Abraham!" "Here I am," he replied.[2]

But the day Lot left Sodom, fire and sulfur rained down from heaven and destroyed them all.[3]

The two *angel*s arrived at Sodom in the evening, and Lot was sitting in the gateway of the city. When he saw them, he got up to meet them and bowed down with his face to the ground.[4]

But in the account of the burning bush, even Moses showed that the dead rise, for he calls the Lord 'the God of Abraham, and the God of Isaac, and the God of Jacob.'[5]

There the *angel* of the Lord appeared to him in flames of fire from within a bush. Moses saw that though the bush was on fire it did not burn up.[6]

So the king gave the order, and they brought Daniel and threw him into the lions' den. The king said to Daniel, "May your God, whom you serve continually, rescue you!"[7]

My God sent his *angel*, and He shut the mouths of the lions. They have not hurt me, because I was found innocent in his sight.[8]

My shield is God Most High, who saves the upright in heart[9].

Then Nebuchadnezzar said, "Praise be to the God of Shadrach, Meshach and Abednego, who has sent his *angel* and rescued his servants!"[10]

They have left the straight way and wandered off to follow the way of Balaam son of Bezer, who loved the wages of wickedness.[11]

Then the Lord opened Balaam's eyes, and he saw the *angel* of the Lord standing in the road with his sword drawn. So he bowed low and fell facedown.[12]

Therefore the Lord himself will give you a sign: The virgin will conceive and give birth to a son, and will call him Immanuel.[13]

In the sixth month of Elizabeth's pregnancy, God sent the *angel* Gabriel to Nazareth, a town in Galilee, to a virgin pledged to be married to a man named Joseph, a descendant of David. The virgin's name was Mary.[14]

Does not Scripture say that the Messiah will come from David's descendants and from Bethlehem, the town where David lived?"[15]

When the *angel*s had left them and gone into heaven, the shepherds said to one another, "Let's go to Bethlehem and see this thing that has happened, which the Lord has told us about."[16]

At the place where Jesus was crucified, there was a garden, and in the garden a new tomb, in which no one had ever been laid.[17]

There was a violent earthquake, for an *angel* of the Lord came down from heaven and, going to the tomb, rolled back the stone and sat on it.[18]

But today I am freeing you from the chains on your wrists.[19]

Suddenly an *angel* of the Lord appeared and a light shone in the cell. He struck Peter on the side and woke him up. "Quick, get up!" he said, and the chains fell off Peter's wrists.[20]

As they traveled along the road, they came to some water and the eunuch said, "Look, here is water. What can stand in the way of my being baptized?"[21]

Now an *angel* of the Lord said to Philip, "Go south to the road— the desert road—that goes down from Jerusalem to Gaza."[22]

For great is the Lord and most worthy of praise; he is to be feared above all gods.[23]

And I saw a mighty *angel* proclaiming in a loud voice, "Who is worthy to break the seals and open the scroll?"[24]

Anger

Do not worship any other god, for the Lord, whose name is Jealous, is a jealous God.[25]

for the Lord your God, who is among you, is a jealous God and his *anger* will burn against you, and he will destroy you from the face of the land.[26]

Therefore, since we are receiving a kingdom that cannot be shaken, let us be thankful, and so worship God acceptably with reverence and awe, for our "God is a consuming fire."[27]

"In the greatness of your majesty you threw down those who opposed you. You unleashed your burning *anger*; it consumed them like stubble.[28]

For God did not appoint us to suffer wrath but to receive salvation through our Lord Jesus Christ.[29]

But for those who are self-seeking and who reject the truth and follow evil, there will be wrath and *anger*.[30]

Jesus entered the temple courts and drove out all who were buying and selling there. He overturned the tables of the money changers and the benches of those selling doves.[31]

If only we knew the power of you *anger*! Your wrath is as great as the fear that is your due.[32]

The chief priests and the whole Sanhedrin were looking for false evidence against Jesus so that they could put him to death.[33]

John saw many Pharisees and Sadducees coming to where he was baptizing. He said to them, "You are like a nest of poisonous snakes! Who warned you to escape the coming of God's *anger*?[34]

The Lord is not slow in keeping his promise, as some understand slowness. Instead He is patient with you, not wanting anyone to perish, but everyone to come to repentance.[35]

And he passed in front of Moses, proclaiming, "The Lord, the Lord, the compassionate and gracious God, slow to *anger*, abounding in love and faithfulness."[36]

Do not let any unwholesome talk come out of your mouths, but only what is helpful for building others up according to their needs, that it may benefit those who listen.[37]

My dear brothers and sisters, take note of this: Everyone should be quick to listen, slow to speak and slow to become angry, because human *anger* does not produce the righteousness that God desires.[38]

Tremble and do not sin; when you are on your beds, search your hearts and be silent.[39]

"In your *anger* do not sin": Do not let the sun go down while you are still angry, and do not give the devil a foothold.[40]

No discipline seems pleasant at the time, but painful. Later on, however, it produces a harvest of righteousness and peace for those who have been trained by it.[41]

Discipline me, Lord, but only in due measure— not in your *anger*, or you will reduce me to nothing.[42]

They tell how you turned to God from idols to serve the living and true God, and to wait for his Son from heaven, whom he raised from the dead—Jesus, who rescues us from the coming wrath.[43]

See, the day of the Lord is coming —a cruel day, with wrath and fierce *anger*— to make the land desolate and destroy the sinners within it.[44]

Coming out of his mouth is a sharp sword with which to strike down the nations. "He will rule them with an iron scepter." He treads the winepress of the fury of the wrath of God Almighty.[45]

Because of their wickedness do not let them escape; in your *anger*, God, bring the nations down.[46]

'He will wipe every tear from their eyes. There will be no more death' or mourning or crying or pain, for the old order of things has passed away."[47]

For his *anger* lasts only a moment, but his favor lasts a lifetime; weeping may stay for the night, but rejoicing comes in the morning.[48]

Apostle

Simon (whom He named Peter), his brother Andrew, James, John, Philip, Bartholomew, Matthew, Thomas, James son of Alphaeus, Simon who was called the Zealot, Judas son of James, and Judas Iscariot, who became a traitor.[49]

The wall of the city had twelve foundations, and on them were the names of the twelve *apostle*s of the Lamb.[50]

It is the Lord your God you must follow, and him you must revere. Keep his commands and obey him; serve him and hold fast to him.[51]

Peter and the other *apostle*s replied: "We must obey God rather than human beings![52]

Let the assembled peoples gather around you, while you sit enthroned over them on high.[53]

The *apostle*s gathered around Jesus and reported to him all they had done and taught.[54]

The angel said to the women, "Do not be afraid, for I know that you are looking for Jesus, who was crucified. He is not here; He has risen, just as he said. Come and see the place where he lay.[55]

They were greatly disturbed because the *apostle*s were teaching the people, proclaiming in Jesus the resurrection of the dead.[56]

I am going to send you what my Father has promised; but stay in the city until you have been clothed with power from on high.[57]

Everyone was filled with awe at the many wonders and signs performed by the *apostle*s.[58]

Blessed are those who act justly, who always do what is right.[59]

They devoted themselves to the *apostles*' teaching and to fellowship, to the breaking of bread and to prayer.[60]

You will be enriched in every way so that you can be generous on every occasion, and through us your generosity will result in thanksgiving to God.[61]

For from time to time those who owned land or houses sold them, brought the money from the sales and put it at the *apostles*' feet, and it was distributed to anyone who had need.[62]

It was about this time that King Herod arrested some who belonged to the church, intending to persecute them. He had James, the brother of John, put to death with the sword.[63]

Because of this, God in his wisdom said, "I will send them prophets and *apostle*s, some of whom they will kill and others they will persecute."[64]

However, if you suffer as a Christian, do not be ashamed, but praise God that you bear that name.[65]

The *apostle*s left the Sanhedrin, rejoicing because they had been counted worthy of suffering disgrace for the Name.[66]

He must become greater; I must become less."[67]

The *apostle*s said to the Lord, "Increase our faith!"[68]

This, then, is how you ought to regard us: as servants of Christ and as those entrusted with the mysteries God has revealed.[69]

And of this gospel I was appointed a herald and an *apostle* and a teacher.[70]

On that day his feet will stand on the Mount of Olives, east of Jerusalem, and the Mount of Olives will be split in two from east to west, forming a great valley, with half of the mountain moving north and half moving south.[71]

Then the *apostle*s returned to Jerusalem from the hill called the Mount of Olives, a Sabbath day's walk from the city.[72]

Believe

"Very truly I tell you," Jesus answered, "before Abraham was born, I am!"[73]

"Do not let your hearts be troubled. You *believe* in God; *believe* also in me.[74]

After he has suffered, he will see the light of life and be satisfied; by his knowledge my righteous servant will justify many, and he will bear their iniquities.[75]

"Yes, Lord," she replied, "I *believe* that you are the Messiah, the Son of God, who is to come into the world."[76]

And let us run with perseverance the race marked out for us, fixing our eyes on Jesus, the pioneer and perfecter of faith. For the joy set before him he endured the cross, scorning its shame, and sat down at the right hand of the throne of God.[77]

This righteousness is given through faith in Jesus Christ to all who *believe*.[78]

He was chosen before the creation of the world, but was revealed in these last times for your sake.[79]

Who has *believe*d our message and to whom has the arm of the LORD been revealed?[80]

Do not be carried away by all kinds of strange teachings.[81]

A simple man *believes* anything, but a prudent man gives thought to his steps.[82]

Come, my children, listen to me; I will teach you the fear of the LORD.[83]

Yet to all who did receive him, to those who *believed* in his name, he gave the right to become children of God-[84]

The god of this age has blinded the minds of unbelievers, so that they cannot see the light of the gospel that displays the glory of Christ, who is the image of God.[85]

But as I told you, you have seen me and still you do not *believe*.[86]

Then will the eyes of the blind be opened and the ears of the deaf unstopped.[87]

When he had gone indoors, the blind men came to him, and he asked them, "Do you *believe* that I am able to do this?" "Yes, Lord," they replied.[88]

You will be his witness to all men of what you have seen and heard.[89]

"You are my witnesses," declares the LORD, "and my servant whom I have chosen, so that you may know and *believe* me and understand that I am he.[90]

He performs wonders that cannot be fathomed, miracles that cannot be counted.[91]

"Unless you people see signs and wonders," Jesus told him, "you will never *believe*."⁹²

Let us discern for ourselves what is right; let us learn together what is good. ⁹³

They said to the woman, "We no longer *believe* just because of what you said; now we have heard for ourselves, and we know that this man really is the Savior of the world."⁹⁴

Therefore, my dear brothers and sisters, stand firm. Let nothing move you. Always give yourselves fully to the work of the Lord, because you know that your labor in the Lord is not in vain.⁹⁵

Jesus answered, "The work of God is this: to *believe* in the one he has sent."⁹⁶

Blood

My heart is in anguish within me; the terrors of death have fallen on me.[97]

And being in anguish, he prayed more earnestly, and his sweat was like drops of *blood* falling to the ground.[98]

But he was pierced for our transgressions, he was crushed for our iniquities; the punishment that brought us peace was on him, and by his wounds we are healed.[99]

For God was pleased to have all his fullness dwell in him, and through him to reconcile to himself all things, whether things on earth or things in heaven, by making peace through his *blood*, shed on the cross.[100]

Blessed is the one whose sin the Lord will never count against them."[101]

To him who loves us and has freed us from our sins by his *blood*, and has made us to be a kingdom and priests to serve his God and Father—to him be glory and power for ever and ever! Amen.[102]

He provided redemption for his people; he ordained his covenant forever— holy and awesome is his name.[103]

In him we have redemption through his *blood*, the forgiveness of sins, in accordance with the riches of God's grace that he lavished on us.[104]

The Lord is near to all who call on him, to all who call on him in truth.[105]

But now in Christ Jesus you who were once far away have been brought near by the *blood* of Christ.[106]

"The days are coming", declares the Lord, "when I will make a new covenant with the people of Israel and with the people of Judah.[107]

In the same way, after supper he took the cup, saying, "This cup is the new covenant in my *blood*; do this, whenever you drink it, in remembrance of me."[108]

Wash away all my iniquity and cleanse me from my sin.[109]

How much more, then, will the *blood* of Christ, who through the eternal Spirit offered himself unblemished to God, cleanse our consciences from acts that lead to death, so that we may serve the living God![110]

The Lord is my shepherd; I lack nothing.[111]

Now may the God of peace, who through the *blood* of the eternal covenant brought back from the dead our Lord Jesus, that great Shepherd of the sheep, equip you with everything good for doing his will, and may he work in us what is pleasing to him, through Jesus Christ, to whom be glory for ever and ever. Amen.[112]

How then can a mortal be righteous before God? How can one born of woman be pure?[113]

Since we have now been justified by his *blood*, how much more shall we be saved from God's wrath through him![114]

"Come now, let us settle the matter," says the Lord. "Though your sins are like scarlet, they shall be as white as snow; though they are red as crimson, they shall be like wool.[115]

And he said, "These are they who have come out of the great tribulation; they have washed their robes and made them white in the *blood* of the Lamb.[116]

And this is the testimony: God has given us eternal life, and this life is in his Son.[117]

Whoever eats my flesh and drinks my *blood* has eternal life, and I will raise them up at the last day.[118]

Born

Do you not know? Have you not heard? The Lord is the everlasting God, the Creator of the ends of the earth.[119]

Before the mountains were *born* or you brought forth the whole world, from everlasting to everlasting you are God.[120]

Then the Lord God made a woman from the rib he had taken out of the man, and he brought her to the man.[121]

For as woman came from man, so also man is *born* of woman. But everything comes from God.[122]

Your eyes saw my unformed body; all the days ordained for me were written in your book before one of them came to be.[123]

"Before I formed you in the womb I knew you, before you were *born* I set you apart;[124]

My times are in your hands;[125]

a time to be *born* and a time to die, a time to plant and a time to uproot,[126]

Indeed, there is no one on earth who is righteous, no one who does what is right and never sins.[127]

"What are mortals, that they could be pure, or those *born* of woman, that they could be righteous?[128]

A shoot will come up from the stump of Jesse; from his roots a Branch will bear fruit.[129]

Today in the town of David a Savior has been *born* to you; he is the Messiah, the Lord.[130]

He is before all things, and in him all things hold together.[131]

"Very truly I tell you," Jesus answered, "before Abraham was *born*, I am!"[132]

Then will the eyes of the blind be opened and the ears of the deaf unstopped.[133]

Nobody has ever heard of opening the eyes of a man *born* blind.[134]

But these are written that you may believe that Jesus is the Messiah, the Son of God, and that by believing you may have life in his name.[135]

Everyone who believes that Jesus is the Christ is *born* of God, and everyone who loves the father loves his child as well.[136]

He saved us through the washing of rebirth and renewal by the Holy Spirit,[137]

Jesus replied, "Very truly I tell you, no one can see the kingdom of God unless they are *born* again."[138]

For the word of God is alive and active. Sharper than any double-edged sword, it penetrates even to dividing soul and spirit, joints and marrow; it judges the thoughts and attitudes of the heart.[139]

For you have been *born* again, not of perishable seed, but of imperishable, through the living and enduring word of God.[140]

How priceless is your unfailing love, O God! People take refuge in the shadow of your wings.[141]

Dear friends, let us love one another, for love comes from God. Everyone who loves has been *born* of God and knows God.[142]

Children

Every good and perfect gift is from above, coming down from the Father of the heavenly lights, who does not change like shifting shadows.[143]

Children are a heritage from the Lord, offspring a reward from him.[144]

The Lord bless you and keep you; the Lord make his face shine on you and be gracious to you; the Lord turn his face toward you and give you peace.[145]

Children's children are a crown to the aged, and parents are the pride of their children.[146]

The fear of the Lord is the beginning of wisdom, and knowledge of the Holy One is understanding.[147]

Come, my children, listen to Me; I will teach you the fear of the Lord.[148]

All Scripture is God-breathed and is useful for teaching, rebuking, correcting and training in righteousness, so that the servant of God may be thoroughly equipped for every good work.[149]

Impress them on your children. Talk about them when you sit at home and when you walk along the road, when you lie down and when you get up.[150]

For God so loved the world that he gave his one and only Son, that whoever believes in him shall not perish but have eternal life.[151]

See what great love the Father has lavished on us, that we should be called *children* of God![152]

Then the sovereignty, power and greatness of all the kingdoms under heaven will be handed over to the holy people of the Most High.[153]

Jesus said, "Let the little *children* come to me, and do not hinder them, for the kingdom of heaven belongs to such as these."[154]

Who among you fears the Lord and obeys the word of his servant? Let the one who walks in the dark, who has no light, trust in the name of the Lord and rely on their God.[155]

Believe in the light while you have the light, so that you may become *children* of light.[156]

Turn from evil and do good; seek peace and pursue it.[157]

Blessed are the peacemakers, for they will be called *children* of God.[158]

Blessed is the one whom God corrects; so do not despise the discipline of the Almighty.[159]

Endure hardship as discipline; God is treating you as his *children*. For what *children* are not disciplined by their father? [160]

Here now is the man who did not make God his stronghold but trusted in his great wealth and grew strong by destroying others!"[161]

The disciples were amazed at his words. But Jesus said again, "*Children*, how hard it is to enter the kingdom of God! It is easier for a camel to go through the eye of a needle than for someone who is rich to enter the kingdom of God."[162]

Even now my witness is in heaven; my advocate is on high.[163]

My dear *children*, I write this to you so that you will not sin. But if anybody does sin, we have an advocate with the Father—Jesus Christ, the Righteous One.[164]

Chosen

The vineyard of the Lord Almighty is the nation of Israel, and the people of Judah are the vines he delighted in.[165]

For the Lord has *chosen* Jacob to be his own, Israel to be his treasured possession.[166]

The God of Abraham, Isaac and Jacob, the God of our fathers, has glorified his servant Jesus.[167]

"Here is my servant, whom I uphold, my *chosen* one in whom I delight; I will put my Spirit on him, and he will bring justice to the nations.[168]

Jesus is "'the stone you builders rejected which has become the cornerstone.'[169]

For in Scripture it says: "See, I lay a stone in Zion, a *chosen* and precious cornerstone, and the one who trusts in him will never be put to shame."[170]

And we have seen and testify that the Father has sent his Son to be the Savior of the world.[171]

The people stood watching, and the rulers even sneered at him. They said, "He saved others; let him save himself if he is God's Messiah, the *Chosen* One."[172]

The people walking in darkness have seen a great light; on those living in the land of deep darkness a light has dawned."[173]

But you are a *chosen* people, a royal priesthood, a holy nation, God's special possession, that you may declare the praises of him who called you out of darkness into his wonderful light.[174]

For those God foreknew he also predestined to be confirmed to the image of his Son, that he might be the firstborn among many brothers and sisters.[175]

"For many are invited, but few are *chosen*."[176]

Therefore, there is now no condemnation for those who are in Christ Jesus,[177]

Who will bring any charge against those whom God has *chosen*? It is God who justifies.[178]

As a prisoner for the Lord, then, I urge you to live a life worthy of the calling you have received. Be completely humble and gentle; be patient, bearing with one another in love.[179]

Therefore, as God's *chosen* people, holy and dear loved, clothe yourselves with compassion, kindness, humility, gentleness, and patience.[180]

For it is better, if it is God's will, to suffer for doing good than for doing evil.[181]

And will not God bring about justice for his *chosen* ones, who cry out to him day and night? Will he keep putting them off?[182]

Sanctify them by the truth; you word is truth.[183]

I have *chosen* the way of faithfulness; I have set my heart on your laws.[184]

"To God belong wisdom and power; counsel and understanding are his.[185]

A voice came from the cloud, saying, "This is my Son, whom I have *chosen*; listen to him.[186]

The armies of heaven were following him, riding on white horses and dressed in fine linen, white and clean.[187]

They will wage war against the Lamb, but the Lamb will triumph over them because he is Lord of lords and King of kings-and with him will be his called, *chosen* and faithful followers."[188]

Create

In the beginning you laid the foundations of the earth, and the heavens are the work of your hands.[189]

In the beginning God *create*d the heavens and the earth.[190]

Acknowledge and take to heart this day that the Lord is God in heaven above and on the earth below. There is no other.[191]

For in him all things were *create*d: things in heaven and on earth, visible and invisible, whether thrones or powers or rulers or authorities; all things have been *create*d through him and for him.[192]

Yours, Lord, is the greatness and the power and the glory and the majesty and the splendor, for everything in heaven and earth is yours. Yours, Lord, is the kingdom; you are exalted as head over all.[193]

"You are worthy, our Lord and God, to receive glory and honor and power, for you *create*d all things, and by your will they were *create*d and have their being."[194]

By the word of the Lord the heavens were made, their starry host by the breath of his mouth.[195]

Lift up your eyes and look to the heavens: Who *create*d all these? He who brings out the starry host one by one and calls forth each of them by name. Because of his great power and mighty strength, not one of them is missing.[196]

When he established the force of the wind and measured out the waters,[197]

He who forms the mountains, who *create*s the wind, and who reveals his thoughts to mankind, who turns dawn to darkness, and treads on the heights of the earth—the Lord God Almighty is his name.[198]

"But at the beginning of creation God 'made them male and female.'[199]

So God *created* mankind in his own image, in the image of God he *create*d them; male and female he *create*d them.[200]

From one man he made all the nations, that they should inhabit the whole earth; and he marked out their appointed times in history and the boundaries of their lands.[201]

For this is what the Lord says—he who *create*d the heavens, he is God; he who fashioned and made the earth, he founded it; he did not *create* it to be empty, but formed it to be inhabited—he says: "I am the Lord, and there is no other.[202]

And the LORD God said, "The man has now become like one of us, knowing good and evil.[203]

You were blameless in your ways from the day you were *created* till wickedness was found in you.[204]

If you declare with your mouth, "Jesus is Lord," and believe in your heart that God raised him from the dead, you will be saved. For it is with your heart that you believe and are justified, and it is with your mouth that you profess your faith and are saved.[205]

Create in me a pure heart, O God, and renew a steadfast spirit within me.[206]

Therefore, if anyone is in Christ, the new creation has come: The old has gone, the new is here![207]

and to put on the new self, *created* to be like God in true righteousness and holiness.[208]

As long as it is day, we must do the works of him who sent me. Night is coming, when no one can work.[209]

For we are God's handiwork, *created* in Christ Jesus to do good works, which God prepared in advance for us to do.[210]

However, as it is written: "What no eye has seen, what no ear has heard, and what no human mind has conceived"—the things God has prepared for those who love him—[211]

"See, I will *create* new heavens and a new earth. The former things will not be remembered, nor will they come to mind.[212]

David

The Most High will thunder from heaven; the LORD will judge the ends of the earth. "He will give strength to his king and exalt the horn of his anointed."[213]

So Samuel took the horn of oil and anointed him in the presence of his brothers, and from that day on the Spirit of the Lord came powerfully upon *David*.[214]

A champion named Goliath, who was from Gath, came out of the Philistine camp. His height was six cubits and a span.[215]

So *David* triumphed over the Philistine with a sling and a stone; without a sword in his hand he struck down the Philistine and killed him.[216]

See how they lie in wait for me! Fierce men conspire against me for no offense or sin of mine, Lord.[217]

Saul sent men to *David*'s house to watch it and to kill him in the morning.[218]

This day you have seen with your own eyes how the Lord delivered you into my hands in the cave.[219]

Then *David* crept up unnoticed and cut off a corner of Saul's robe.[220]

"I have installed my King on Zion, my holy mountain."[221]

Nevertheless, *David* captured the fortress of Zion—which is the City of David.[222]

The man said, "She is Bathsheba, the daughter of Eliam and the wife of Uriah the Hittite."[223]

Then *David* said to Nathan, "I have sinned against the Lord."[224]

Lord, how many are my foes! How many rise up against me![225]

A messenger came and told *David*, "The hearts of the people of Israel are with Absalom."[226]

The king was shaken. He went up to the room over the gateway and wept. As he went, he said: "O my son Absalom! My son, my son Absalom! If only I had died instead of you—O Absalom, my son, my son!"[227]

The king asked the man from Cush, "Is the young man Absalom safe?" The man replied, "King *David*, may your enemies be like that young man. May all those who rise up to harm you be like him."[228]

I said, "Have mercy on me, Lord; heal me, for I have sinned against you."[229]

***David* was conscience-stricken after he had counted the fighting men, and he said to the Lord, "I have sinned greatly in what I have done. Now, Lord, I beg you, take away the guilt of your servant. I have done a very foolish thing.**[230]

Zadok the priest took the horn of oil from the sacred tent and anointed Solomon. Then they sounded the trumpet and all the people shouted, "Long live King Solomon!"[231]

So Solomon sat on the throne of the Lord as king in place of his father *David*.[232]

He died at a good old age, having enjoyed long life, wealth and honor.[233]

"Now when *David* had served God's purpose in his own generation, he fell asleep; he was buried with his ancestors and his body decayed.[234]

Their leader will be one of their own; their ruler will arise from among them.[235]

Afterward the Israelites will return and seek the Lord their God and *David* their king. They will come trembling to the Lord and to his blessings in the last days.[236]

Eternal

In the beginning God created the heavens and the earth.[237]

For since the creation of the world God's invisible qualities—his *eternal* power and divine nature—have been clearly seen, being understood from what has been made, so that men are without excuse.[238]

On his robe and on his thigh he has this name written: KING OF KINGS AND LORD OF LORDS.[239]

Now to the King *eternal*, immortal, invisible, the only God, be honor and glory for ever and ever. Amen.[240]

Truly he is my rock and my salvation; he is my fortress, I will never be shaken.[241]

Trust in the LORD forever, for the LORD, the LORD himself , is the Rock *eternal*.[242]

For great is the LORD and most worthy of praise; he is to be feared above all gods.[243]

The fear of the LORD is the beginning of wisdom; all who follow his precepts have good understanding. To him belongs *eternal* praise.[244]

The mind governed by the flesh is death, but the mind governed by the Spirit is life and peace.[245]

Whoever sows to please their flesh, from the flesh will reap destruction; whoever sows to please the Spirit, from the Spirit will reap *eternal* life.[246]

"The multitude of your sacrifices— what are they to me?" says the Lord. "I have more than enough of burnt offerings, of rams and the fat of fattened animals; I have no pleasure in the blood of bulls and lambs and goats.[247]

He did not enter by means of the blood of goats and calves; but he entered the Most Holy Place once for all by his own blood, thus obtaining *eternal* redemption.[248]

For what I received I passed on to you as of first importance: that Christ died for our sins according to the Scriptures, that he was buried, that he was raised on the third day according to the Scriptures,[249]

Then I saw another angel flying in midair, and he had the *eternal* gospel to proclaim to those who live on the earth —to every nation, tribe, language and people.[250]

what is mankind that you are mindful of them, human beings that you care for them?[251]

You have made known to me the path of life; you will fill me with joy in your presence, with *eternal* pleasures at your right hand.[252]

I consider that our present sufferings are not worth comparing with the glory that will be revealed in us.[253]

For our light and momentary troubles are achieving for us an *eternal* glory that far outweighs them all.[254]

The Word became flesh and made his dwelling among us. We have seen his glory, the glory of the one and only Son, who came from the Father, full of grace and truth.[255]

Your word, Lord, is *eternal*; it stands firm in the heavens.[256]

Faith

Though you have not seen him, you love him; and even though you do not see him now, you believe in him and are filled with an inexpressible and glorious joy.[257]

Now *faith* is confidence in what we hope for and assurance about what we do not see.[258]

I would like to learn just one thing from you: Did you receive the Spirit by the works of the law, or by believing what you heard?[259]

Consequently, *faith* comes from hearing the message, and the message is heard through the word about Christ.[260]

He is the Rock, his works are perfect, and all his ways are just.[261]

Therefore, since we are surrounded by such a great cloud of witnesses, let us throw off everything that hinders and the sin that so easily entangles. And let us run with perseverance the race marked out for us, fixing our eyes on Jesus, the pioneer and perfecter of *faith*.[262]

For God did not appoint us to suffer wrath but to receive salvation through our Lord Jesus Christ.[263]

For it is by grace you have been saved, through *faith*—and this is not from yourselves, it is the gift of God—[264]

Some time later God tested Abraham. He said to him, "Abraham!" "Here I am," he replied. Then God said, "Take your son, your only son, whom you love—Isaac—and go to the region of Moriah.

Sacrifice him there as a burnt offering on a mountain I will show you."[265]

These have come so that the proven genuineness of your *faith*—of greater worth than gold, which perishes even though refined by fire—may result in praise, glory and honor when Jesus Christ is revealed.[266]

But Moses said to God, "Who am I that I should go to Pharaoh and bring the Israelites out of Egypt?"[267]

He replied, "You of little *faith*, why are you so afraid?"[268]

David said to Goliath, "You are coming to fight against me with a sword, a spear and a javelin. But I'm coming against you in the name of the Lord who rules over all."[269]

Be on your guard; stand firm in the *faith*; be courageous; be strong.[270]

The king was overjoyed and gave orders to lift Daniel out of the den. And when Daniel was lifted from the den, no wound was found on him, because he had trusted in his God.[271]

Guard my life, for I am *faith*ful to you; save your servant who trusts in you. You are my God.[272]

Great is our Lord and mighty in power; his understanding has no limit.[273]

My message and my preaching were not with wise and persuasive words, but with a demonstration of the Spirit's

power, so that your *faith* might not rest on human wisdom, but on God's power.[274]

While they were stoning him, Stephen prayed, "Lord Jesus, receive my spirit."[275]

I have fought the good fight, I have finished the race, I have kept the *faith*.[276]

Be alert and of sober mind. Your enemy the devil prowls around like a roaring lion looking for someone to devour.[277]

In addition to all this, take up the shield of *faith*, with which you can extinguish all the flaming arrows of the evil one.[278]

They called out in a loud voice, "How long, Sovereign Lord, holy and true, until you judge the inhabitants of the earth and avenge our blood?"[279]

I tell you, he will see that they get justice, and quickly. However, when the Son of Man comes, will he find *faith* on the earth?"[280]

Forgive

I, even I, am he who blots out your transgressions, for my own sake, and remembers your sins more.[281]

For I will *forgive* their wickedness and will remember their sins no more."[282]

Truly my soul finds rest in God; my salvation comes from him.[283]

Who can *forgive* sins but God alone?[284]

"The days are coming," declares the Lord, "when I will make a new covenant with the people of Israel and with the people of Judah.[285]

This is my blood of the covenant, which is poured out for many for the *forgive*ness of sins.[286]

But now in Christ Jesus you who once were far away have been brought near by the blood of Christ.[287]

In fact, the law requires that everything be cleansed with blood, and without the shedding of blood there is no *forgive*ness.[288]

But he was pierced for our transgressions, he was crushed for our iniquities; the punishment that brought us peace was on him, and by his wounds we are healed.[289]

"Blessed are they whose transgressions are *forgive*n, whose sins are covered.[290]

They divide my clothes among them and cast lots for my garment.[291]

Jesus said, "Father, *forgive* them, for they do not know what they are doing." And they divided up his clothes by casting lots.[292]

She will give birth to a son, and you are to give him the name Jesus, because he will save his people from their sins."[293]

Help us, God our Savior, for the glory of your name; deliver us and *forgive* our sins for your name's sake.[294]

If you declare with your mouth "Jesus is Lord", and believe in your heart that God raised him from the dead, you will be saved.[295]

I am writing to you, dear children, because your sins have been *forgive*n on account of his name.[296]

The Lord is not slow in keeping his promise, as some understand slowness. Instead he is patient with you, not wanting anyone perish, but everyone to come to repentance.[297]

Peter replied, "Repent and be baptized, every one of you, in the name of Jesus Christ for the *forgive*ness of your sins.[298]

Then I acknowledged my sin to you and did not cover up my iniquity. I said, "I will confess my transgressions to the Lord." And you forgave the guilt of my sin.[299]

If we confess our sins, he is faithful and just and will *forgive* us our sins and purify us from all unrighteousness.[300]

A person's wisdom yields patience; it is to one's glory to overlook an offense.[301]

Bear with each other and *forgive* one another if any of you has a grievance against someone. *Forgive* as the Lord forgave you.[302]

Nothing in all creation is hidden from God's sight. Everything is uncovered and laid bare before the eyes of him to whom we must give account.[303]

But who can discern their own errors? *Forgive* my hidden faults.[304]

Free

For the wages of sin is death, but the gift of God is eternal life in Christ Jesus our Lord.[305]

And the Lord God commanded the man, "You are *free* to eat from any tree in the garden; but you must not eat from the tree of the knowledge of good and evil, for when you eat from it you will certainly die."[306]

What a wretched man I am! Who will rescue me from this body that is subject to death?[307]

So if the Son sets you *free*, you will be *free* indeed.[308]

For Christ also suffered once for sins, the righteous for the unrighteous, to bring you to God. He was put to death in the body but made alive in the Spirit.[309]

But now he has reconciled you by Christ's physical body through death to present you holy in his sight, without blemish and *free* from accusation—[310]

Who is it that overcomes the world? Only the one who believes that Jesus is the Son of God.[311]

Through him everyone who believes is set *free* from every sin,[312]

For the Lord your God is God of gods and Lord of lords, the great God, mighty and awesome, who shows no partiality and accepts no bribes.[313]

There is neither Jew nor Gentile, neither slave nor *free*, nor is there male and female, for you are all one in Christ Jesus.[314]

Jesus answered, "I am the way and the truth and the life. No one comes to the Father except through me.[315]

Then you will know the truth, and the truth will set you *free*.[316]

Religion that God our Father accepts as pure and faultless is this: to look after orphans and widows in their distress and to keep oneself from being polluted by the world.[317]

They have *free*ly scattered their gifts to the poor, their righteousness endures forever; their horn will be lifted high in honor.[318]

Command them to do good, to be rich in good deeds, and to be generous and willing to share.[319]

Good will come to those who are generous and lend *free*ly, who conduct their affairs with justice.[320]

Each of you should use whatever gift you have received to serve others, as faithful stewards of God's grace in its various forms.[321]

You, my brothers and sisters, were called to be *free*. But do not use your *free*dom to indulge the flesh; rather, serve one another humbly in love.[322]

For the love of money is a root of all kinds of evil. Some people, eager for money, have wandered from the faith and pierced themselves with many griefs.[323]

Keep your lives *free* from the love of money and be content with what you have, because God has said, "Never will I leave you; never will I forsake you."[324]

For, "Whoever would love life and see good days must keep their tongue from evil and their lips from deceitful speech.[325]

Keep your mouth *free* of perversity; keep corrupt talk far from your lips.[326]

Jesus answered her, "If you knew the gift of God and who it is that asks you for a drink, you would have asked him and he would have given you living water."[327]

The Spirit and the bride say, "Come!" And let the one who hears say, "Come!" Let the one who is thirsty come; and let the one who wishes take the *free* gift of the water of life.[328]

God

I am the Alpha and the Omega, the First and the Last, the Beginning and the End.[329]

Before the mountains were born or you brought forth the whole world, from everlasting to everlasting you are *God*.[330]

Your eyes are too pure to look on evil; you cannot tolerate wrongdoing.[331]

Exalt the Lord our *God* and worship at his holy mountain, for the Lord our *God* is holy.[332]

I the Lord do not change. So you, the descendants of Jacob, are not destroyed.[333]

Because *God* wanted to make the unchanging nature of his purpose very clear to the heirs of what was promised, he confirmed it with an oath.[334]

"I know that you can do all things; no purpose of yours can be thwarted.[335]

Then I heard what sounded like a great multitude, like the roar of rushing waters and like peals of thunder, shouting: "Hallelujah! For the Lord *God* Almighty reigns.[336]

Who can hide in secret places so that I cannot see them?" declares the Lord. "Do not I fill heaven and earth?" declares the Lord.[337]

"But will *God* really dwell on earth? The heavens, even the highest heaven, cannot contain you. How much less this temple I have built![338]

Great is our Lord and mighty in power; his understanding has no limit.[339]

If our hearts condemns us, we know that *God* is greater than our hearts, and he knows everything.[340]

You are good, and what you do is good; teach me your decrees.[341]

"Why do you call me good?" Jesus Answered. "No one is good—but *God* alone.[342]

But I trust in your unfailing love; my heart rejoices in your salvation.[343]

Whoever does not love does not know *God*, because *God* is love.[344]

Though you have made me see troubles, many and bitter, you will restore my life again; from the depths of the earth you will again bring me up.[345]

And the *God* of all grace, who called you to his eternal glory in Christ, after you have suffered a little while, will himself restore you and make you strong, firm and steadfast.[346]

I said, "Have mercy on me, Lord; heal me, for I have sinned against you."[347]

But because of his great love for us, *God*, who is rich in mercy, made us alive with Christ even when we were dead in transgressions—it is by grace you have been saved.[348]

Then you will call on me and come and pray to me, and I will listen to you.[349]

The smoke of the incense, together with the prayers of *God*'s people, went up before *God* from the angel's hand.[350]

The Word became flesh and made his dwelling among us.[351]

And I heard a loud voice from the throne saying, "Look! *God*'s dwelling place is now among the people, and he will dwell with them. They will be his people, and *God* himself will be with them and be their *God*.[352]

Great

"I am the Alpha and the Omega," says the Lord God, "who is, and who was, and who is to come, the Almighty."[353]

How *great* is God—beyond our understanding! The number of his years is past finding out.[354]

I am the Lord your God; consecrate yourselves and be holy, because I am holy.[355]

Your ways, God, are holy. What god is as *great* as our God?[356]

But God is my King from long ago; he brings salvation on the earth.[357]

For the LORD is the *great* God, the *great* King above all gods.[358]

All the nations may walk in the name of their gods, but we will walk in the name of the Lord our God for ever and ever.[359]

My name will be *great* among the nations, from where the sun rises to where it sets.[360]

"I called to the Lord, who is worthy of praise, and have been saved from my enemies.[361]

For *great* is the LORD and most worthy of praise; he is to be feared above all gods.[362]

Give thanks to the God of heaven. His love endures forever.[363]

"Lord, the *great* and awesome God, who keeps his covenant of love with those who love him and keep his commandments,[364]

I say to the Lord, "You are my God." Hear, Lord, my cry for mercy."[365]

David said to Gad, "I am in deep distress. Let us fall into the hands of the Lord, for his mercy is *great*; but do not let me fall into human hands."[366]

Jesus answered, "It is written: 'Worship the Lord your God and serve him only.' "[367]

Ezra praised the Lord, the *great* God; and all the people lifted their hands and responded, "Amen! Amen!" Then they bowed down and worshipped the Lord with their faces to the ground.[368]

Good and upright is the Lord; therefore he instructs sinners in his ways.[369]

Then Levi held a *great* banquet for Jesus at his house, and a large crowd of tax collectors and others were eating with them.[370]

When they had finished eating, Jesus said to Simon Peter, "Simon son of John, do you love me more than these?" "Yes, Lord," he said, "you know that I love you." Jesus said, "Feed my lambs."[371]

When Jesus looked up and saw a *great* crowd coming toward him, he said to Philip, "Where shall we buy bread for these people to eat?"[372]

He was oppressed and afflicted, yet he did not open his mouth; he was led like a lamb to the slaughter, and as a sheep before its shearers is silent, so he did not open his mouth.[373]

But Jesus made no reply, not even to a single charge—to the *great* amazement of the governor.[374]

The Lord looks down from heaven on all mankind to see if there are any who understand, any who seek God.[375]

Therefore, since we have a *great* high priest who has ascended into heaven, Jesus the Son of God, let us hold firmly to the faith we profess.[376]

Heaven

Praise him, sun and moon; praise him, all you shining stars. Let them praise the name of the Lord, for at his command they were created,[377]

By the word of the LORD the *heavens* were made, their starry host by the breath of his mouth.[378]

All your works praise you, Lord; your faithful people extol you.[379]

The *heavens* declare the glory of God; the skies proclaim the work of his hands.[380]

A father to the fatherless, a defender of widows, is God in his holy dwelling.[381]

My help comes from the LORD, the Maker of *heaven* and earth.[382]

"To him who sits on the throne and to the Lamb be praise and honor and glory and power, for ever and ever!"[383]

The LORD has established his throne in *heaven*, and his kingdom rules over all.[384]

And we have seen and testify that the Father has sent his Son to be the Savior of the world.[385]

And a voice from *heaven* said, "This is my Son, whom I love; with him I am well pleased."[386]

"Now have come the salvation and the power and the kingdom of our God, and the authority of his Messiah.[387]

From that time on Jesus began to preach, "Repent, for the kingdom of *heaven* has come near."[388]

Simon Peter answered him, "Lord, to whom shall we go? You have the words of eternal life.[389]

Whom have I in *heaven* but you? And earth has nothing I desire besides you.[390]

Since, then, you have been raised with Christ, set your hearts on things above, where Christ is, seated at the right hand of God.[391]

Do not store up for yourselves treasures on earth, where moths and vermin destroy, and where thieves break in and steal. But store up for yourselves treasures in *heaven*, where moths and vermin do not destroy, and where thieves do not break in and steal.[392]

so is my word that goes out from my mouth: It will not return to me empty, but will accomplish what I desire and achieve the purpose for which I sent it.[393]

***Heaven* and earth will pass away, but my words will never pass away.[394]**

For as lightning that comes from the east is visible even in the west, so will be the coming of the Son of Man.[395]

"In my vision at night I looked, and there before me was one like a son of man, coming with the clouds of *heaven*.[396]

Coming out of his mouth is a sharp sword with which to strike down the nations. "He will rule them with an iron scepter." He treads the winepress of the fury of the wrath of God Almighty.[397]

The wrath of God is being revealed from *heaven* against all godlessness and wickedness of people, who suppress the truth by their wickedness,[398]

However, as it is written: "What no eye has seen, what no ear has heard, and what no human mind has conceived"—the things God has prepared for those who love him—[399]

"See, I will create new *heaven*s and a new earth. The former things will not be remembered, nor will they come to mind.[400]

Holy

Your eyes are too pure to look on evil; you cannot tolerate wrongdoing.[401]

Each of the four living creatures had six wings and was covered with eyes all around, even under its wings. Day and night they never stop saying: "*Holy, holy, holy* is the Lord God Almighty,' who was and is and is to come"[402]

Praise him, all his angels; praise him, all his heavenly hosts.[403]

In the council of the *holy* ones God is greatly feared; he is more awesome than all who surround him.[404]

"Nazareth! Can anything good come from there?" Nathanael asked.[405]

"What do you want with us, Jesus of Nazareth? Have you come to destroy us? I know who you are—the *Holy* One of God!"[406]

He anointed us, set his seal of ownership on us, and put his Spirit in our hearts as a deposit, guaranteeing what is to come.[407]

When you believed, you were marked in him with a seal, the promised *Holy* Spirit, who is a deposit guaranteeing our inheritance until the redemption of those who are God's possession—to the praise of his glory.[408]

And this is love: that we walk in obedience to his commands.[409]

The Lord will establish you as his *holy* people, as he promised you on oath, if you keep the commands of the Lord your God and walk in his obedience to him.[410]

When Jesus spoke again to the people, he said, "I am the light of the world. Whoever follows me will never walk in darkness, but will have the light of life."[411]

But you are a chosen people, a royal priesthood, a *holy* nation, God's special possession, that you may declare the praises of him who called you out of darkness into his wonderful light.[412]

But from now on, the Son of Man will be seated at the right hand of the mighty God."[413]

God reigns over the nations; God is seated on his *holy* throne.[414]

Then Peter said, "Silver or gold I do not have, but what I have I give you. In the name of Jesus Christ of Nazareth, walk."[415]

Stretch out your hand to heal and perform signs and wonders through the name of your *holy* servant Jesus.[416]

Do not conform to the pattern of this world, but be transformed by the renewing of your mind.[417]

For God did not call us to be impure, but to live a *holy* life.[418]

"Sacrifice thank offerings to God, fulfill your vows to the Most High,[419]

Therefore, I urge you, brothers and sisters, in view of God's mercy, to offer your bodies as a living sacrifice, *holy* and pleasing to God—this is your true and proper worship.[420]

Sing the glory of his name; make his praise glorious.[421]

Glory in his *holy* name; let the hearts of those who seek the Lord rejoice.[422]

Hope

Be on your guard; stand firm in the faith; be courageous; be strong.[423]

Be strong and take heart, all you who *hope* in the Lord.[424]

Take my yoke upon you and learn from me, for I am gentle and humble in heart, and you will find rest for your souls.[425]

Yes, my soul, find rest in God; my *hope* comes from him.[426]

They tell of the power of your awesome works—and I will proclaim your great deeds.[427]

You answer us with awesome and righteous deeds, God our Savior, the *hope* of all the ends of the earth and of the farthest seas,[428]

"Every word of God is flawless; he is a shield to those who take refuge in him.[429]

We wait in *hope* for the Lord; He is our help and our shield.[430]

For the word of the Lord is right and true; he is faithful in all he does.[431]

You are my refuge and my shield; I have put my *hope* in your word.[432]

May your unfailing love come to me, Lord, your salvation, according to your promise;[433]

Sustain me, my God, according to your promise, and I will live; do not let my *hope*s be dashed.[434]

Let everything that has breath praise the Lord.[435]

Why, my soul, are you downcast? Why so disturbed within me? Put your *hope* in God, for I will yet praise him, my Savior and my God.[436]

Therefore my heart is glad and my tongue rejoices; my body also will rest secure,[437]

You will be secure, because there is *hope*; you will look about you and take your rest in safety.[438]

Therefore God exalted him to the highest place and gave him the name that is above every name, that at the name of Jesus every knee should bow, in heaven and on earth and under the earth.[439]

In his name the nations will put their *hope*."[440]

Jesus replied, "Very truly I tell you, no one can see the kingdom of God unless they are born again."[441]

Praise be to the God and Father of our Lord Jesus Christ! In his great mercy he has given us new birth into a living *hope* through the resurrection of Jesus Christ from the dead,[442]

Better a little with the fear of the Lord than great wealth with turmoil.[443]

Command those who are rich in this present world not to be arrogant nor to put their *hope* in wealth, which is so uncertain, but to put their *hope* in God, who richly provides us with everything for our enjoyment.[444]

Let your conversation be always full of grace, seasoned with salt, so that you may know how to answer everyone.[445]

Always be prepared to give an answer to everyone who asks you to give the reason for the *hope* that you have.[446]

Jacob

In the womb he grasped his brother's heel; as a man he struggled with God.[447]

After this, his brother came out, with his hand grasping Esau's heel; so he was named *Jacob*.[448]

See that no one is sexually immoral, or is godless like Esau, who for a single meal sold his inheritance rights as the oldest son.[449]

But *Jacob* said, "Swear to me first." So he swore an oath to him, selling his birthright to *Jacob*.[450]

Enemies disguise themselves with their lips, but in their hearts they harbor deceit.[451]

***Jacob* said to his father, "I am Esau your firstborn. I have done as you told me. Please sit up and eat some of my game, so that you may give me your blessing."[452]**

Love is patient, love is kind.[453]

***Jacob* was in love with Rachel and said, "I'll work for you seven years in return for your younger daughter Rachel."[454]**

All these are the twelve tribes of Israel, and this is what their father said to them when he blessed them, giving each the blessing appropriate to him.[455]

***Jacob* had twelve sons:[456]**

He struggled with the angel and overcame him; he wept and begged for his favor.[457]

Then the man said, "Your name will no longer be *Jacob*, but Israel, because you have struggled with God and with humans and have overcome."[458]

Save me, I pray, from the hand of my brother Esau, for I am afraid he will come and attack me, and also the mothers with their children.[459]

But Esau ran to meet *Jacob* and embraced him; he threw his arms around his neck and kissed him. And they wept.[460]

Do not take revenge, my friends, but leave room for God's wrath, for it is written: "It is mine to avenge; I will repay," says the Lord.[461]

Three days later, while all of them were still in pain, two of *Jacob*'s sons, Simeon and Levi, Dinah's brothers, took their swords and attacked the unsuspecting city, killing every male.[462]

As she breathed her last—for she was dying—she named her son Ben-Oni. But his father named him Benjamin.[463]

Over her tomb *Jacob* set up a pillar, and to this day that pillar marks Rachel's tomb.[464]

Now Israel loved Joseph more than any of his other sons, because he had been born to him in his old age; and he made a richly ornamented robe for him.[465]

With your mighty arm you redeemed your people, the descendants of *Jacob* and Joseph.[466]

Then he gave them these instructions: "I am about to be gathered to my people. Bury me with my fathers in the cave in the field of Ephron the Hittite,"[467]

'I am the God of Abraham, the God of Isaac, and the God of Jacob'? He is not the God of the dead but of the living."[468]

Jesus

Therefore the Lord himself will give you a sign: The virgin will conceive and give birth to a son, and will call him Immanuel.[469]

This is how the birth of *Jesus* the Messiah came about: His mother Mary was pledged to be married to Joseph, but before they came together, she was found to be pregnant through the Holy Spirit.[470]

The Spirit of the Lord will rest on him—the spirit of wisdom and understanding, the spirit of counsel and might, the spirit of knowledge and the fear of the Lord—[471]

As soon as *Jesus* was baptized, he went up out of the water. At that moment heaven was opened, and he saw the Spirit of God descending like a dove and alighting on him.[472]

For we do not have a high priest who is unable to empathize with our weaknesses, but we have one who has been tempted in every way, just as we are—yet he did not sin.[473]

***Jesus*, full of the Holy Spirit, left the Jordan and was led by the Spirit into the wilderness, where for forty days he was tempted by the devil.[474]**

To the Israelites the glory of the LORD looked like a consuming fire on top of the mountain.[475]

After six days *Jesus* took with Him Peter, James and John the brother of James, and led them up a high mountain by themselves. There he was transfigured before them. His face shone like the sun, and his clothes became as white as the light.[476]

Very truly I tell you, a time is coming and has now come when the dead will hear the voice of the Son of God and those who hear will live.[477]

When he had said this, *Jesus* called in a loud voice, "Lazarus, come out!" The dead man came out, his hands and feet wrapped with strips of linen, and a cloth around his face.[478]

From the ends of the earth we hear singing: "Glory to the Righteous One." But I said, "I waste away, I waste away! Woe to me! The treacherous betray! With treachery the treacherous betray!"[479]

When evening came, *Jesus* was reclining at the table with the Twelve. And while they were eating, he said, "Truly I tell you, one of you will betray me."[480]

But he was pierced for our transgressions, he was crushed for our iniquities; the punishment that brought us peace was on him, and by his wounds we are healed.[481]

***Jesus* called out with a loud voice, "Father, into your hands I commit my spirit." When he had said this, he breathed his last.**[482]

For to be sure, he was crucified in weakness, yet he lives by God's power.[483]

"Don't be alarmed," he said. "You are looking for *Jesus* the Nazarene, who was crucified. He has risen! He is not here. See the place where they laid him.[484]

He was given authority, glory and sovereign power; all nations and peoples of every language worshiped him.[485]

Then *Jesus* came to them and said, "All authority in heaven and on earth has been given to me. Therefore go and make disciples of all nations, baptizing them in the name of the Father and of the Son and of the Holy Spirit,"[486]

After he said this, he was taken up before their very eyes, and a cloud hid him from their sight.[487]

***Jesus* said, "I am with you for only a short time, and then I am going to the one who sent me."[488]**

At that time they will see the Son of Man coming in a cloud with power and great glory.[489]

That's how we should live as we wait for the blessed hope God has given us. We are waiting for *Jesus* Christ to appear in all his glory. He is our great God and Savior.[490]

Then I saw "a new heaven and a new earth," for the first heaven and the first earth had passed away, and there was no longer any sea.[491]

Now this is eternal life: that they know you, the only true God, and *Jesus* Christ, whom you have sent.[492]

Joseph

"Before I formed you in the womb I knew you, before you were born I set you apart;[493]

Then God remembered Rachel; he listened to her and enabled her to conceive. She became pregnant and gave birth to a son and said, "God has taken away my reproach." She named him *Joseph*, and said, "May the Lord add to me another son."[494]

Anger is cruel and fury overwhelming, but who can stand before jealousy?[495]

So when *Joseph* came to his brothers, they stripped him of his robe—the ornate robe he was wearing— and they took him and threw him into the cistern.[496]

"You have heard that it was said, 'You shall not commit adultery.' But I tell you that anyone who looks at a woman lustfully has already committed adultery with her in his heart.[497]

and after a while his master's wife took notice of *Joseph* and said, "Come to bed with me!"[498]

For the Lord God is a sun and shield; the Lord bestows favor and honor; no good thing does he withhold from those whose walk is blameless.[499]

But while *Joseph* was there in the prison, the Lord was with him; he showed him kindness and granted him favor in the eyes of the prison warden.[500]

But whoever lives by the truth comes into the light, so that it may be seen plainly that what they have done has been done in the sight of God.[501]

Pharaoh said to *Joseph*, "I had a dream, and no one can interpret it. But I have heard it said of you that when you hear a dream you can interpret it."[502]

The Lord rewards everyone for their righteousness and faithfulness.[503]

So Pharaoh said to *Joseph*, "I hereby put you in charge of the whole land of Egypt."[504]

This is the way he governs the nations and provides food in abundance.[505]

***Joseph* collected all the food produced in those seven years of abundance in Egypt and stored it in the cities.[506]**

In times of disaster they will not wither; in days of famine they will enjoy plenty.[507]

The seven years of abundance in Egypt came to an end, and the seven years of famine began, just as *Joseph* had said.[508]

People curse the one who hoards grain, but they pray God's blessing on the one who is willing to sell.[509]

Now *Joseph* was the governor of the land, the person who sold grain to all its people. So when *Joseph*'s brothers arrived, they bowed down to him with their faces to the ground.[510]

For this son of mine was dead and is alive again; he was lost and is found.' So they began to celebrate.[511]

Israel said to *Joseph*, "Now I am ready to die, since I have seen for myself that you are still alive."[512]

"I know that you can do all things; no purpose of yours can be thwarted.[513]

But *Joseph* said to them, "Don't be afraid. Am I in the place of God? You intended to harm me, but God intended it for good to accomplish what is now being done, the saving of many lives.[514]

"This is the same Moses they had rejected with the words, 'Who made you ruler and judge?' He was sent to be their ruler and deliverer by God himself, through the angel who appeared to him in a bush.[515]

Then *Joseph* said to his brothers, "I am about to die. But God will surely come to your aid and take you up out of this land to the land he promised on oath to Abraham, Isaac and Jacob."[516]

Joy

The heavens declare the glory of God; the skies proclaim the work of his hands.[517]

For you make me glad by your deeds, Lord; I sing for *joy* at what your hands have done.[518]

Thus the heavens and the earth were completed in all their vast array.[519]

Shout for *joy* to God, all the earth![520]

Blessed are those who have learned to acclaim you, who walk in the light of your presence, Lord.[521]

Surely you have granted him unending blessings and made him glad with the *joy* of your presence.[522]

Therefore, just as sin entered the world through one man, and death through sin, and in this way death came to all people, because all sinned—[523]

Grieve, mourn and wail. Change your laughter to mourning and your *joy* to gloom.[524]

The Son is the radiance of God's glory and the exact representation of his being, sustaining all things by his powerful word. After he had provided purification for sins, he sat down at the right hand of the Majesty in heaven.[525]

Shouts of *joy* and victory resound in the tents of the righteous: "The LORD's right hand has done mighty things!"526

They all ate the same spiritual food and drank the same spiritual drink; for they drank from the spiritual rock that accompanied them, and that rock was Christ.527

Come, let us sing for *joy* to the LORD; let us shout aloud to the Rock of our salvation.528

For where your treasure is, there your heart will be also.529

The kingdom of heaven is like treasure hidden in a field. When a man found it, he hid it again, and then in his *joy* went and sold all he had and bought that field.530

Therefore, since we are receiving a kingdom that cannot be shaken, let us be thankful, and so worship God acceptably with reverence and awe.531

Worship the LORD with gladness; come before him with *joy*ful songs.532

I instruct you in the way of wisdom and lead you along straight paths.533

You have made known to me the paths of life; you will fill me with *joy* in your presence.'534

Blessed are those who are persecuted because of righteousness, for theirs is the kingdom of heaven.535

Consider it pure *joy*, my brothers and sisters, whenever you face trials of many kinds because you know that the testing of your faith produces perseverance.[536]

For by one sacrifice he has made perfect forever those who are being made holy.[537]

To him who is able to keep you from stumbling and to present you before his glorious presence without fault and with great *joy*
—[538]

Kingdom

"How great you are, Sovereign LORD! There is no one like you, and there is no God but you, as we have heard with our own ears.[539]

"'Our Father in heaven, hallowed be your name, your *kingdom* come, your will be done, on earth as it is in heaven.[540]

Let them know that you, whose name is the LORD— that you alone are the Most High over all the earth.[541]

"Lord Almighty, the God of Israel, enthroned between the cherubim, you alone are God over all the *kingdom*s of the earth.[542]

Save us and help us with your right hand, that those you love may be delivered.[543]

Now, LORD our God, deliver us from his hand, so that all *kingdom*s on earth may know that you alone, LORD, are God."[544]

Sing to the LORD, for he has done glorious things; let this be known to all the world.[545]

Sing to God, you *kingdom*s of the earth, sing praises to the Lord,[546]

For the Lord takes delight in his people; he crowns the humble with victory. [547]

Blessed are the poor in spirit, for theirs is the *kingdom* of heaven.[548]

We are hard pressed on every side, but not crushed; perplexed, but not in despair; persecuted, but not abandoned; struck down, but not destroyed.[549]

Blessed are those who are persecuted because of righteousness, for theirs is the *kingdom* of heaven.[550]

The LORD is near to all who call on him, to all who call on him in truth.[551]

As you go, proclaim this message: 'The *kingdom* of heaven is near'[552]

Truly I tell you, if you have faith as small as a mustard seed, you can say to this mountain, 'Move from here to there,' and it will move.[553]

"The *kingdom* of heaven is like a mustard seed, which a man took and planted in his field.[554]

Then they understood that he was not telling them to guard against the yeast used in bread, but against the teaching of the Pharisees and Sadducees.[555]

"The *kingdom* of heaven is like yeast that a woman took and mixed with three measures of flour until all the dough had risen."[556]

I will give you hidden treasures, riches stored in secret places, so that you may know that I am the Lord, the God of Israel, who summons you by name. [557]

"The *kingdom* of heaven is like treasure hidden in a field.[558]

All the nations will be gathered before him, and he will separate the people one from another as a shepherd separates the sheep from the goats.[559]

"Once again, the *kingdom* of heaven is like a net that was let down into the lake and caught all kinds of fish. When it was full, the fisherman pulled it up on the shore. Then they sat down and collected the good fish in baskets, but threw the bad away.[560]

The world and its desires pass away, but whoever does the will of God lives forever.[561]

**"Not everyone who says to me, 'Lord, Lord,' will enter the *kingdom* of Heaven, but only the one who does the will of my Father who is in heaven. **[562]

Labor

The Lord is my shepherd, I lack nothing.[563]

"Consider how the wild flowers grow. They do not *labor* or spin. Yet I tell you, not even Solomon in all his splendor was dressed like one of these.[564]

For the creation was subjected to frustration, not by its own choice, but by the will of the one who subjected it, in hope that the creation itself will be liberated from its bondage to decay and brought into the freedom and glory of the children of God.[565]

He named him Noah and said, "He will comfort us in the *labor* and painful toil of our hands caused by the ground the Lord has cursed."[566]

There remains, then, a Sabbath-rest for the people of God; for anyone who enters God's rest also rests from their works, just as God did from his.[567]

Six days you shall *labor* and do all your work, but the seventh day is a sabbath to the Lord your God.[568]

Be very careful, then, how you live—not as unwise but as wise, making the most of every opportunity, because the days are evil.[569]

This is what I have observed to be good: that it is appropriate for a person to eat, to drink and to find satisfaction in their toilsome *labor* under the sun during the few days of life God has given them—for this is their lot.[570]

By the sweat of your brow you will eat your food until you return to the ground, since from it you were taken; for dust you are and to dust you will return."[571]

Then people go out to their work, to their *labor* until evening.[572]

Tell the righteous it will be well with them, for they will enjoy the fruit of their deeds.[573]

You will eat the fruit of your *labor*; blessings and prosperity will be yours.[574]

As iron sharpens iron, so one person sharpens another.[575]

Two are better than one, because they have a good return for their *labor*: If either of them falls down, one can help the other up.[576]

For no one can lay any foundation other than the one already laid, which is Jesus Christ.[577]

Unless the Lord builds the house, the builders *labor* in vain.[578]

But as for you, be strong and do not give up, for your work will be rewarded."[579]

Therefore, my dear brothers and sisters, stand firm. Let nothing move you. Always give yourselves fully to the work of the Lord, because you know that your *labor* in the Lord is not in vain.[580]

For the Son of Man is going to come in his Father's glory with his angels, and then he will reward each person according to what they have done.[581]

What do people gain from all their *labor*s at which they toil under the sun?[582]

Laugh

From their callous hearts comes iniquity; their evil imaginations have no limits. They scoff, and speak with malice; with arrogance they threaten oppression.[583]

The One enthroned in heaven *laugh*s; the Lord scoffs at them.[584]

The proud and arrogant person—"Mocker" is his name—behaves with insolent fury.[585]

but the Lord *laugh*s at the wicked, for he knows their day is coming.[586]

I have heard a message from the Lord; an envoy was sent to the nations to say, "Assemble yourselves to attack it! Rise up for battle!"[587]

But you *laugh* at them, Lord; you scoff at all those nations.[588]

May the God of hope fill you with all joy and peace as you trust in him, so that you may overflow with hope by the power of the Holy Spirit.[589]

He will yet fill your mouth with *laugh*ter and your lips with shouts of joy.[590]

Jesus replied, "What is impossible with man is possible with God."[591]

Abraham fell facedown; he *laugh*ed and said to himself, "Will a son be born to a man a hundred years old? Will Sarah bear a child at the age of ninety?"592

Now you, brothers and sisters, like Isaac, are children of promise.593

Sarah said, "God has brought me *laugh*ter, and everyone who hears about this will *laugh* with me."594

For although they knew God, they neither glorified him as God nor gave thanks to him, but their thinking became futile and their foolish hearts were darkened.595

Grieve, mourn and wail. Change your *laugh*ter to mourning and your joy to gloom.596

Blessed is the one who does not condemn himself by what he approves.597

Even in *laugh*ter the heart may ache, and rejoicing may end in grief.598

Rejoice with those who rejoice; mourn with those who mourn.599

a time to weep and a time to *laugh*, a time to mourn and a time to dance,600

May the Lord answer you when you are in distress; may the name of the God of Jacob protect you.601

You will *laugh* at destruction and famine, and need not fear the wild animals.[602]

Then people will say, Surely the righteous still are rewarded; surely there is a God who judges the earth."[603]

Blessed are you who hunger now, for you will be filled. Blessed are you who weep now, for you will *laugh*.[604]

Light

For he spoke, and it came to be; he commanded, and it stood firm.[605]

And God said, "Let there be *light*," and there was *light*."[606]

The sun has one kind of splendor, the moon another and the stars another; and star differs from star in splendor.[607]

God made two great *light*s—the greater *light* to govern the day and the lesser *light* to govern the night. He also made the stars.[608]

The Spirit of God has made me; the breath of the Almighty gives me life.[609]

Look on me and answer, Lord my God. Give *light* to my eyes, or I will sleep in death,[610]

For you created my inmost being; you knit me together in my mother's womb.[611]

The human spirit is the lamp of the Lord that sheds *light* on one's inmost being.[612]

But the way of the wicked is like deep darkness; they do not know what makes them stumble.[613]

The god of this age has blinded the minds of unbelievers, so that they cannot see the *light* of the gospel that displays the glory of Christ, who is the image of God.[614]

Today in the town of David a Savior has been born to you; he is the Messiah, the Lord.[615]

the people living in darkness have seen a great *light;* on those living in the land of the shadow of death a *light* has dawned."[616]

Jesus answered, "I am the way and the truth and the life. No one comes to the Father except through me.[617]

"What is the way to the abode of *light*?[618]

Praise be to the Lord, to God our Savior, who daily bears our burdens.[619]

For my yoke is easy and my burden is *light*."[620]

You will surely forget your trouble, recalling it only as waters gone by.[621]

For our *light* and momentary troubles are achieving for us an eternal glory that far outweighs them all.[622]

Each of you should use whatever gift you have received to serve others, as faithful stewards of God's grace in its various forms.[623]

Every good and perfect gift is from above, coming down from the Father of the heavenly *light*s, who does not change like shifting shadows.[624]

You have made known to me the paths of life; you will fill me with joy in your presence.'[625]

Blessed are those who have learned to acclaim you, who walk in the *light* of your presence, Lord.[626]

But who can endure the day of his coming? Who can stand when he appears? For he will be like a refiner's fire or a launderer's soap.[627]

their work will be shown for what it is, because the Day will bring it to *light*. It will be revealed with fire, and the fire will test the quality of each person's work.[628]

Lord

As you do not know the path of the wind, or how the body is formed in a mother's womb, so you cannot understand the work of God, the Maker of all things.[629]

He who forms the mountains, who creates the wind, and who reveals his thoughts to mankind, who turns dawn to darkness, and treads on the heights of the earth—the *Lord* God Almighty is his name.[630]

Like your name, O God, your praise reaches to the ends of the earth; your right hand is filled with righteousness.[631]

I will give thanks to the *Lord* because of his righteousness; I will sing the praises of the name of the *Lord* Most High.[632]

Before the mountains were born or you brought forth the whole world, from everlasting to everlasting you are God.[633]

Do you not know? Have you not heard? The *Lord* is the everlasting God, the Creator of the ends of the earth.[634]

Command those who are rich in this present world not to be arrogant nor to put their hope in wealth, which is so uncertain, but to put their hope in God, who richly provides us with everything for our enjoyment.[635]

So Abraham called that place The *LORD* Will Provide. And to this day it is said, "On the mountain of the *LORD* it will be provided."[636]

Let him lead me to the banquet hall, and let his banner over me be love.[637]

Moses built an altar and called it The *LORD* is my Banner.[638]

"Glory to God in the highest heaven, and on earth peace to those on whom his favor rests."[639]

So Gideon built an altar to the *LORD* there and called it The *LORD* is Peace.[640]

I will sing a new song to you, my God; on the ten-stringed lyre I will make music to you, to the One who gives victory to kings, who delivers his servant David.[641]

David said to the Philistine, "You come against me with sword and spear and javelin, but I come against you in the name of the *Lord* Almighty, the God of the armies of Israel, whom you have defied.[642]

For the Lamb at the center of the throne will be their shepherd; 'he will lead them to springs of living water.'[643]

The *LORD* is my shepherd, I lack nothing.[644]

It is because of him that you are in Christ Jesus, who has become for us wisdom from God—that is, our righteousness, holiness and redemption.[645]

In his days Judah will be saved and Israel will live in safety. This is the name by which he will be called: The *Lord* Our Righteousness Savior.[646]

I saw the Holy City, the new Jerusalem, coming down out of heaven from God, prepared as a bride beautifully dressed for her husband.[647]

"The distance all around will be 18,000 cubits. "And the name of the city from that time on will be: THE *LORD* IS THERE."[648]

Love

And we have seen and testify that the Father has sent his Son to be the Savior of the world.[649]

For God so *loved* the world that he gave his one and only Son, that whoever believes in him shall not perish but have eternal life.[650]

For God was pleased to have all his fullness dwell in him,[651]

And a voice from heaven said, "This is my Son, whom I *love*; with him I am well pleased."[652]

But the way of the wicked is like deep darkness; they do not know what makes them stumble.[653]

This is the verdict: Light has come into the world, but people *loved* darkness instead of light because their deeds were evil.[654]

When Jesus spoke again to the people, he said, "I am the light of the world. Whoever follows me will never walk in darkness, but will have the light of life."[655]

For he has rescued us from the dominion of darkness and brought us into the kingdom of the Son he *loves*,[656]

for all have sinned and fall short of the glory of God,[657]

But God demonstrates his own *love* for us in this: While we were still sinners, Christ died for us.[658]

God presented Christ as a sacrifice of atonement, through the shedding of his blood—to be received by faith.[659]

This is *love*: not that we *love*d God, but that he *love*d us and sent his Son as an atoning sacrifice for our sins.[660]

When he had received the drink, Jesus said, "It is finished." With that, he bowed his head and gave up his spirit.[661]

This is how we know what *love* is: Jesus Christ laid down his life for us.[662]

As Jesus started on his way, a man ran up to him and fell on his knees before him. "Good teacher," he asked, "what must I do to inherit eternal life?"[663]

Everyone who believes that Jesus is the Christ is born of God, and everyone who *loves* the father *loves* his child as well.[664]

For it is by grace you have been saved, through faith—and this is not from yourselves, it is the gift of God—not by works, so that no one can boast.[665]

The life I now live in the body, I live by faith in the Son of God, who *love*d me and gave himself for me.[666]

All Scripture is God-breathed and is useful for teaching, rebuking, correcting and training in righteousness, so that the servant of God may be thoroughly equipped for every good work.[667]

But if anyone obeys his word, *love* for God is truly made complete in them.[668]

Endure hardship as discipline; God is treating you as his children. For what children are not disciplined by their father? [669]

My son, do not despise the Lord's discipline, and do not resent his rebuke, because the Lord disciplines those he *love*s, as a father the son he delights in.[670]

After that, we who are still alive and are left will be caught up together with them in the clouds to meet the Lord in the air. And so we will be with the Lord forever.[671]

Surely your goodness and *love* will follow me all the days of my life, and I will dwell in the house of the Lord forever.[672]

Majesty

Who is this, robed in splendor, striding forward in the greatness of his strength?[673]

Splendor and *majesty* are before him; strength and glory are in his sanctuary.[674]

For who in the skies above can compare with the LORD? Who is like the LORD among the heavenly beings?[675]

Proclaim the power of God, whose *majesty* is over Israel, whose power is in the heavens.[676]

He is the Rock, his works are perfect, and all his ways are just. A faithful God who does no wrong, upright and just is he.[677]

They speak of the glorious splendor of your *majesty*—and I will meditate on your wonderful works.[678]

Our God comes and will not be silent; a fire devours before him, and around him a tempest rages.[679]

And you said, "The Lord our God has shown us his glory and his *majesty*, and we have heard his voice from the fire.[680]

When they heard this, they raised their voices together in prayer to God. "Sovereign Lord," they said, "you made the heaven and the earth and the sea, and everything in them.[681]

They raise their voices, they shout for joy; from the west they acclaim the LORD's *majesty*.[682]

He who made the Pleiades and Orion, who turns midnight into dawn and darkens day into night, who calls for the waters of the sea and pours them out over the face of the land—the Lord is his name.[683]

Yours, Lord, is the greatness and the power and the glory and the *majesty* and the splendor, for everything in heaven and earth is yours.[684]

For the grace of God has appeared that offers salvation to all people.[685]

But when grace is shown to the wicked, they do not learn righteousness; even in a land of uprightness they go on doing evil and do not regard the *majesty* of the Lord.[686]

We have seen his glory, the glory of the One and only Son, who came from the Father, full of grace and truth.[687]

For we did not follow cleverly devised stories when we told you about the coming of our Lord Jesus Christ in power, but we were eyewitnesses of his *majesty*.[688]

When he had received the drink, Jesus said, "It is finished." With that, he bowed his head and gave up his spirit.[689]

The Son is the radiance of God's glory and the exact representation of his being, sustaining all things by his powerful word. After he had provided purification for sins, he sat down at the right hand of the *Majesty* in heaven.[690]

They called to the mountains and the rocks, "Fall on us and hide us from the face of him who sits on the throne and from the wrath of the Lamb!691

People will flee to caves in the rocks and to holes in the ground from the fearful presence of the Lord and the splendor of his *majesty*, when he rises to shake the earth.692

I saw heaven standing open and there before me was a white horse, whose rider is called Faithful and True. With justice he judges and makes war.693

In your *majesty* ride forth victoriously in the cause of truth, humility and justice; let your right hand achieve awesome deeds.694

The righteous will inherit the land and dwell in it forever.695

to the only God our Savior be glory, *majesty*, power and authority, through Jesus Christ our Lord, before all ages, now and forevermore! Amen.696

Mercy

Religion that God our Father accepts as pure and faultless is this: to look after widows and orphans in their distress and to keep oneself being polluted by the world.[697]

For I desire *mercy*, not sacrifice, and acknowledgment of God rather than burnt offerings.[698]

But from everlasting to everlasting the LORD's love is with those who fear him, and his righteousness with their children's children —[699]

His *mercy* extends to those who fear him, from generation to generation.[700]

All of us have become like one who is unclean, and all our righteous acts are like filthy rags; we all shrivel up like a leaf, and like the wind our sins sweep us away.[701]

he saved us, not because of righteous things we had done, but because of his *mercy*. He saved us through the washing of rebirth and renewal by the Holy Spirit.[702]

Heal me, LORD, and I will be healed; save me and I will be saved, for you are the one I praise.[703]

I said, "Have *mercy* on me, Lord; heal me, for I have sinned against you."[704]

"I, even I, am he who blots out your transgressions, for my own sake, and remembers your sins no more.[705]

Have *mercy* on me, O God, according to your unfailing love; according to your great compassion blot out my transgressions.[706]

If you declare with your mouth, "Jesus is Lord," and believe in your heart that God raised him from the dead, you will be saved.[707]

Whoever conceals their sins does not prosper, but the one who confesses and renounces them finds *mercy*.[708]

Jesus replied, "Very truly I tell you, no one can see the kingdom of God unless they are born again.[709]

Praise be to the God and Father of our Lord Jesus Christ! In his great *mercy* he has given us new birth into a living hope through the resurrection of Jesus Christ from the dead, and into an inheritance that can never perish, spoil or fade.[710]

The Lord is not slow in keeping his promise, as some understand slowness. Instead he is patient with you, not wanting anyone to perish, but everyone to come to repentance.[711]

But for that very reason I was shown *mercy* so that in me, the worst of sinners, Christ Jesus might display his immense patience as an example for those who would believe in him and receive eternal life.[712]

This is the confidence we have in approaching God: that if we ask anything according to his will, he hears us.[713]

Let us then approach God's throne of grace with confidence, so that we may receive *mercy* and find grace to help us in our time of need.[714]

Do you not know that your bodies are members of Christ himself?[715]

Therefore, I urge you, brothers and sisters, in view of God's *mercy*, to offer your bodies as a living sacrifice, holy and pleasing to God—this is your true and proper worship.[716]

How abundant are the good things that you have stored up for those who fear you, that you bestow in the sight of all, on those who take refuge in you.[717]

***Mercy*, peace and love be yours in abundance.**[718]

Moses

"He reached down from on high and took hold of me; he drew me out of deep waters.[719]

When the child grew older, she took him to Pharaoh's daughter and he became her son. She named him *Moses*, saying, "I drew him out of the water."[720]

He makes winds his messengers, flames of fire his servants.[721]

There the angel of the LORD appeared to him in flames of fire from within a bush. *Moses* saw that though the bush was on fire it did not burn up.[722]

He prepared a path for his anger; he did not spare them from death but gave them over to the plague.[723]

Now the Lord had said to *Moses*, "I will bring one more plague on Pharaoh and on Egypt. After that, he will let you go from here, and when he does, he will drive you out completely.[724]

By faith the people passed through the Red Sea as on dry land; but when the Egyptians tried to do so, they were drowned.[725]

***Moses* answered the people, "Do not be afraid. Stand firm and you will see the deliverance the Lord will bring you today. The Egyptians you see today you will never see again.[726]**

This is the bread that came down from heaven. Your ancestors ate manna and died, but whoever feeds on this bread will live forever."[727]

Then the Lord said to *Moses*, "I will rain down bread from heaven for you.[728]

He declared to you his covenant, the Ten Commandments, which he commanded you to follow and then wrote them on two stone tablets.[729]

When the Lord finished speaking to *Moses* on Mount Sinai, he gave him the two tablets of the covenant law, the tablets of stone inscribed by the finger of God.[730]

Remember this and never forget how you aroused the anger of the Lord your God in the wilderness.[731]

When the people saw that *Moses* was so long in coming down from the mountain, they gathered around Aaron and said, "Come, make us gods who will go before us.[732]

"Arise, shine, for your light has come, and the glory of the LORD rises upon you.[733]

When *Moses* came down from Mount Sinai with the two tablets of the covenant law in his hands, he was not aware that his face was radiant because he had spoken with the Lord.[734]

They grumbled in their tents and did not obey the LORD.[735]

The Lord said to *Moses*, "Make a snake and put it up on a pole; anyone who is bitten can look at it and live."[736]

Therefore, you will see the land only from a distance; you will not enter the land I am giving to the people of Israel."[737]

Then the Lord said to *Moses*, "Go up this mountain in the Abarim Range and see the land I have given the Israelites.[738]

"I am now a hundred and twenty years old and I am no longer able to lead you.[739]

And *Moses* the servant of the Lord died there in Moab, as the Lord had said.[740]

After six days Jesus took Peter, James and John with him and led them up a high mountain, where they were all alone. There he was transfigured before them.[741]

Two men, *Moses* and Elijah, appeared in glorious splendor, talking with Jesus.[742]

Nothing

In the beginning God created the heavens and the earth.[743]

"Ah, Sovereign Lord, you have made the heavens and the earth by your great power and outstretched arm. *Nothing* is too hard for you.[744]

"You are worthy, our Lord and God, to receive glory and honor and power, for you created all things, and by your will they were created and have their being."[745]

Through him all things were made; without him *nothing* was made that has been made.[746]

All people will fear; they will proclaim the works of God and ponder what he has done.[747]

I know that everything God does will endure forever; *nothing* can be added to it and *nothing* taken from it. God does it so that people will fear him.[748]

The Lord saw how great the wickedness of the human race had become on the earth, and that every inclination of the thoughts of the human heart was only evil all the time.[749]

The perverse of heart shall be far from me; I will have *nothing* to do with what is evil.[750]

This is how the birth of Jesus the Messiah came about: His mother Mary was pledged to be married to Joseph, but before they came together, she was found to be pregnant through the Holy Spirit.[751]

Who, being in very nature God, did not consider equality with God something to be used to his own advantage; rather, he made himself *nothing* by taking the very nature of a servant, being made in human likeness.[752]

"Isn't this the carpenter's son? Isn't his mother's name Mary, and aren't his brothers James, Joseph, Simon and Judas? Aren't all his sisters with us? Where then did this man get all these things?" And they took offense at him.[753]

He grew up before him like a tender shoot, and like a root out of dry ground. He had no beauty or majesty to attract us to him, *nothing* in his appearance that we should desire him.[754]

For you know that it was not with perishable things such as silver or gold that you were redeemed from the empty way of life handed down to you from your ancestors, but with the precious blood of Christ, a lamb without blemish or defect.[755]

For this is what the Lord says: "You were sold for *nothing*, and without money you will be redeemed."[756]

When he had received the drink, Jesus said, "It is finished." With that, he bowed his head and gave up his spirit.[757]

After the sixty-two 'sevens,' the Anointed One will be put to death and will have *nothing*.[758]

The god of this age has blinded the minds of unbelievers, so that they cannot see the light of the gospel that displays the glory of Christ, who is the image of God.[759]

They know *nothing*, they understand *nothing*; their eyes are plastered over so they cannot see, and their minds closed so they cannot understand.[760]

Jesus answered, "I am the way and the truth and the life. No one comes to the Father except through me.[761]

"I am the vine; you are the branches. If you remain in me and I in you, you will bear much fruit; apart from me you can do *nothing*.[762]

For we must all appear before the judgment seat of Christ, so that each of us may receive what is due us for the things done while in the body, whether good or bad.[763]

***Nothing* in all creation is hidden from God's sight. Everything is uncovered and laid bare before the eyes of him to whom we must give account.**[764]

David Rhodes

Peace

I am the Alpha and the Omega, the First and the Last, the Beginning and the End.[765]

Grace to you and *peace* from him who is, and who was, and who is to come,[766]

Who is he, this King of glory? The LORD Almighty—he is the King of glory.[767]

 "Blessed is the king who comes in the name of the Lord!" "*Peace* in heaven and glory in the highest!"[768]

No harm overtakes the righteous, but the wicked have their fill of trouble.[769]

"There is no *peace*," says the LORD, "for the wicked."[770]

Let the wicked forsake their ways and the unrighteous their thoughts. Let them turn to the Lord, and he will have mercy on them, and to our God, for he will freely pardon.[771]

Turn from evil and do good; seek *peace* and pursue it.[772]

I confess my iniquity; I am troubled by my sin.[773]

***Peace* I leave with you; my *peace* I give you. I do not give to you as the world gives. Do not let your hearts be troubled and do not be afraid.[774]**

For it is with your heart that you believe and are justified, and it is with your mouth that you profess your faith and are saved.[775]

Therefore, since we have been justified through faith, we have *peace* with God through our Lord Jesus Christ.[776]

This is the confidence we have in approaching God: that if we ask anything according to his will, he hears us.[777]

Eli answered, "Go in *peace*, and may the God of Israel grant you what you have asked of him."[778]

For the entire law is fulfilled in keeping this one command: "Love your neighbor as yourself."[779]

If it is possible, as far as it depends on you, live at *peace* with everyone.[780]

Sing to God, you kingdoms of the earth, sing praise to the Lord.[781]

You will go out in joy and be led forth in *peace*; the mountains and hills will burst into song before you, and all the trees of the field will clap their hands.[782]

Let us not become weary in doing good, for at the proper time we will reap a harvest if we do not give up.[783]

Peacemakers who sow in *peace* reap a harvest of righteousness.[784]

His kingdom is an eternal kingdom; his dominion endures from generation to generation.[785]

Of the greatness of his government and *peace* there will be no end.[786]

The Son is the radiance of God's glory and the exact representation of his being, sustaining all things by his powerful word. After he had provided purification for sins, he sat down at the right hand of the Majesty in heaven.[787]

For God was pleased to have all his fullness dwell in him, and through him to reconcile to himself all things, whether things on earth or things in heaven, by making *peace* through his blood, shed on the cross.[788]

Power

He says, "Be still, and know that I am God; I will be exalted among the nations, I will be exalted in the earth."[789]

"God is exalted in his *power*. Who is a teacher like him? [790]

Nothing in all creation is hidden from God's sight. Everything is uncovered and laid bare before the eyes of him to whom we must give account.[791]

For since the creation of the world God's invisible qualities—his eternal *power* and divine nature—have been clearly seen, being understood from what has been made, so that people are without excuse.[792]

for all have sinned and fall short of the glory of God,[793]

The sting of death is sin, and the *power* of sin is the law.[794]

Be alert and of sober mind. Your enemy the devil prowls around like a roaring lion looking for someone to devour.[795]

Since the children have flesh and blood, he too shared in their humanity so that by his death he might break the *power* of him who holds the *power* of death—that is, the devil — [796]

In his great mercy he has given us new birth into a living hope through the resurrection of Jesus Christ from the dead,[797]

I want to know Christ—yes, to know the *power* of his resurrection and participation in his sufferings, becoming like him in his death,[798]

And I will ask the Father, and he will give you another advocate to help you and be with you forever—[799]

For the Spirit God gave us does not make us timid, but gives us *power*, love and self-discipline.[800]

All Scripture is God-breathed and is useful for teaching, rebuking, correcting and training in righteousness,[801]

In this way the word of the Lord spread widely and grew in *power*.[802]

Whoever is ashamed of me and of my words, the Son of Man will be ashamed of them when he comes in his glory and in the glory of the Father and of the holy angels.[803]

For I am not ashamed of the gospel, because it is the *power* of God that brings salvation to everyone who believes: first to the Jew, then to the Gentile.[804]

We know that God does not listen to sinners. He listens to the godly person who does his will.[805]

The prayer of a righteous man is *power*ful and effective.[806]

God chose the weak things of the world to shame the strong.[807]

But he said to me, "My grace is sufficient for you, for my *power* is made perfect in weakness."808

Remember that you molded me like clay. Will you now turn me to dust again?809

But we have this treasure in jars of clay to show that this all-surpassing *power* is from God and not from us.810

"Look, he is coming with the clouds," and "every eye will see him, even those who pierced him"; and all the peoples of the earth "will mourn because of him." So shall it be! Amen.811

At that time they will see the Son of Man coming in a cloud with *power* and great glory.812

Praise

God said to Moses, "I am who I am.[813]

Praise be to the LORD, the God of Israel, from everlasting to everlasting. Amen and Amen.[814]

This is the account of the heavens and the earth when they were created, when the Lord God made the earth and the heavens.[815]

"Praise be to the Lord, the God of Israel, who made heaven and earth![816]

Then the Lord God formed the man from the dust of the ground and breathed into his nostrils the breath of life, and the man became a living being.[817]

I praise you, because I am fearfully and wonderfully made;[818]

As for you, you were dead in your transgressions and sins,[819]

Among the dead no one proclaims your name. Who praises you from the grave?[820]

They all asked, "Are you then the Son of God?" He replied, "You say that I am."[821]

Praise be to the God and Father of our Lord Jesus Christ, who has blessed us in the heavenly realms with every spiritual blessing in Christ.[822]

and who through the Spirit of holiness was appointed the Son of God in power by his resurrection from the dead: Jesus Christ our Lord.[823]

The LORD lives! *Praise* **be to my Rock! Exalted be God my Savior!**[824]

For you have been born again, not of perishable seed, but of imperishable, through the living and enduring word of God.[825]

Praise **be to the God and Father of our Lord Jesus Christ! In his great mercy he has given us new birth into a living hope through the resurrection of Jesus Christ from the dead,**[826]

Rejoice in the LORD and be glad, you righteous; sing, all you who are upright in heart![827]

Sing to God, sing in *praise* **of his name, extol him who rides on the clouds; rejoice before him—his name is the Lord.**[828]

But the eyes of the LORD are on those who fear him, on those whose hope is in his unfailing love,[829]

Then a voice came from the throne, saying: "*Praise*** our God, all you his servants, you who fear him, both great and small!"**[830]

Love the LORD your God with all your heart and with all your soul and with all your strength.[831]

I will *praise* **you, Lord my God, with all my heart; I will glorify your name forever.**[832]

May these words of my mouth and this meditation of my heart be pleasing in your sight, LORD, my Rock and my Redeemer.[833]

Accept, Lord, the willing *praise* of my mouth, and teach me your laws.[834]

Pray

If your enemy is hungry, give him food to eat; if he is thirsty, give him water to drink.[835]

But I tell you, love your enemies and *pray* for those who persecute you,[836]

Do not think of yourself more highly than you ought, but rather think of yourself with sober judgment, in accordance with the faith God has distributed to each of you.[837]

"And when you *pray*, do not be like the hypocrites, for they love to *pray* standing in the synagogues and on the street corners to be seen by others. Truly I tell you, they have received their reward in full.[838]

The eyes of the Lord are on the righteous, and his ears are attentive to their cry;[839]

But when you *pray*, go into your room, close the door and *pray* to your Father, who is unseen. Then your Father, who sees what is done in secret, will reward you.[840]

Do not be quick with your mouth, do not be hasty in your heart to utter anything before God. God is in heaven and you are on earth, so let your words be few.[841]

And when you *pray*, do not keep on babbling like pagans, for they think they will be heard because of their many words.[842]

For this is what the high and exalted One says—he who lives forever, whose name is holy: "I live in a high and holy place, but also with the one who is contrite and lowly in spirit, to revive the spirit of lowly and to revive the heart of the contrite.[843]

This then, is how you should *pray*: "Our Father in heaven, hallowed be your name,[844]

When the woman saw that the fruit of the tree was good for food and pleasing to the eye, and also desirable for gaining wisdom, she took some and ate it.[845]

Watch and *pray* so that you will not fall into temptation. The spirit is willing, but the flesh is weak."[846]

"Tell us what we should say to him; we cannot draw up our case because of darkness.[847]

In the same way, the Spirit helps us in our weakness. We do not know what we ought to *pray* for, but the Spirit himself intercedes for us through wordless groans.[848]

Will they find delight in the Almighty? Will they call on God at all times?[849]

And *pray* in the Spirit on all occasions with all kinds of *prayers* and requests. With this in mind, be alert and always keep on *pray*ing for all the Lord's people.[850]

Hear my cry for mercy as I call to you for help, as I lift up my hands toward your Most Holy Place.[851]

Therefore I want the men everywhere to *pray*, lifting up holy hands without anger or disputing.[852]

When I am in distress, I call to you, because you answer me.[853]

Is anyone among you in trouble? Let him *pray*. Is anyone happy? Let him sing songs of praise.[854]

They drove out many demons and anointed many sick people with oil and healed them.[855]

Is anyone among you sick? Let them call the elders of the church to *pray* over them and anoint them with oil in the name of the Lord.[856]

We know that God does not listen to sinners. He listens to the godly person who does his will.[857]

Therefore confess your offenses to each other and *pray* for each other so that you may be healed. The *prayer* of a righteous person is powerful and effective.[858]

Rest

"You are worthy, our Lord and God, to receive glory and honor and power, for you created all things, and by your will they were created and have their being"[859]

Then God blessed the seventh day and made it holy, because on it he *rested* from all the work of creating that he had done.[860]

Though you have not seen him, you love him; and even though you do not see him now, you believe in him and are filled with an inexpressible and glorious joy, for you are receiving the end result of your faith, the salvation of your souls.[861]

Truly my soul finds *rest* in God; my salvation comes from him.[862]

The Son is the radiance of God's glory and the exact representation of his being, sustaining all things by his powerful word. After he had provided purification for sins, he sat down at the right hand of the Majesty in heaven.[863]

Let your hand *rest* on the man at your right hand, the son of man you have raised up for yourself.[864]

But when he, the Spirit of truth, comes, he will guide you into all the truth. He will not speak on his own; he will speak only what he hears, and he will tell you what is yet to come.[865]

My message and my preaching were not with wise and persuasive words, but with a demonstration of the Spirit's power, so that your faith might not *rest* on human wisdom, but on God's power.[866]

When he comes, he will prove the world to be in the wrong about sin and righteousness and judgment:[867]

I have no peace, no quietness; I have no *rest*, but only turmoil."[868]

Be completely humble and gentle; be patient, bearing with one another in love.[869]

Take my yoke upon you and learn from me, for I am gentle and humble in heart, and you will find *rest* for your souls.[870]

I will refresh the weary and satisfy the faint."[871]

"Come to me, all you who are weary and burdened, and I will give you *rest*.[872]

But the wicked are like the tossing sea, which cannot rest, whose waves cast up mire and mud.[873]

For they cannot *rest* until they do evil; they are robbed of sleep till they make someone stumble.[874]

They claim to know God, but by their actions they deny him. They are detestable, disobedient and unfit for doing anything good.[875]

And to whom did God swear that they would never enter his *rest* if not to those who disobeyed?[876]

I can do all things through him who gives me strength.[877]

But he said to me, "My grace is sufficient for you, for my power is made perfect in weakness." Therefore I will boast all the more gladly about my weaknesses, so that Christ's power may *rest* on me.[878]

Therefore, "they are before the throne of God and serve him day and night in his temple; and he who sits on the throne will shelter them with his presence.[879]

Whoever dwells in the shelter of the Most High will *rest* in the shadow of the Almighty.[880]

Righteous

I, the LORD, speak the truth; I declare what is right.[881]

The Lord is *righteous* in all his ways and faithful in all he does.[882]

The precepts of the Lord are right, giving joy to the heart.[883]

You are *righteous*, Lord, and your laws are right.[884]

for the Mighty One has done great things for me—holy is his name.[885]

Your *righteous*ness, God, reaches to the heavens, you who have done great things. Who is like you, God?[886]

For God is the King of all the earth; sing to him a psalm of praise.[887]

Like your name, O God, your praise reaches to the ends of the earth; your right hand is filled with *righteous*ness.[888]

Here is a trustworthy saying that deserves full acceptance: Christ Jesus came into the world to save sinners—of whom I am the worst.[889]

On hearing this, Jesus said to them, "It is not the healthy who need a doctor, but the sick. I have not come to call the *righteous*, but sinners." [890]

Awake, and rise to my defense! Contend for me, my God and Lord.[891]

My dear children, I write this to you so that you will not sin. But if anybody does sin, we have an advocate with the Father—Jesus Christ, the *Righteous* One.[892]

My spirit is broken, my days are cut short, the grave awaits me.[893]

For through the Spirit we eagerly await by faith the *righteous*ness for which we hope.[894]

Then Jesus asked, "What is the kingdom of God like? What shall I compare it to?[895]

For the kingdom of God is not a matter of eating and drinking, but of *righteous*ness, peace and joy in the Holy Spirit,[896]

"Every word of God is flawless; he is a shield to those who take refuge in him.[897]

All your words are true; all your *righteous* laws are eternal.[898]

He replied, "Blessed rather are those who hear the word of God and obey it."[899]

May my tongue sing of your word, for all your commands are *righteous*.[900]

All the nations will be gathered before him, and he will separate the people one from another as a shepherd separates the sheep from the goats.[901]

This is how it will be at the end of the age. The angels will come and separate the wicked from the *righteous*.[902]

For the wages of sin is death, but the gift of God is eternal life in Christ Jesus our Lord.[903]

Then the *righteous* will shine like the sun in the kingdom of their Father. Whoever has ears, let them hear.[904]

Sacrifice

In fact, the law requires that nearly everything be cleansed with blood, and without the shedding of blood there is no forgiveness.[905]

I will *sacrifice* fat animals to you and an offering of rams; I will offer bulls and goats.[906]

Everyone who sins breaks the law; in fact, sin is lawlessness.[907]

***Sacrifice* a bull each day as a sin offering to make atonement.[908]**

"Remember, Lord, how I have walked before you faithfully and with wholehearted devotion and have done what is good in your eyes." [909]

Then God said, "Take your son, your only son, whom you love—Isaac—and go to the region of Moriah. *Sacrifice* him there as a burnt offering on a mountain I will show you."[910]

"I have more than enough of burnt offerings, of rams and the fat of fattened animals; I have no pleasure in the blood of bulls and lambs and goats.[911]

To love him with all your heart, with all your understanding and with all your strength, and to love your neighbor as yourself is more important than all burnt offerings and *sacrifices*."[912]

It is impossible for the blood of bulls and goats to take away sins.[913]

And by that will, we have been made holy through the *sacrifice* of the body of Jesus Christ once for all.[914]

Whoever does not love does not know God, because God is love.[915]

This is love: not that we loved God, but that he loved us and sent his Son as an atoning *sacrifice* for our sins.[916]

To him who loves us and has freed us from our sins by his blood, and has made us to be a kingdom and priests to serve his God and Father—to him be glory and power for ever and ever![917]

you also, like living stones, are being built into a spiritual house, to be a holy priesthood, offering spiritual *sacrifice*s acceptable to God through Jesus Christ.[918]

Do you not know that your bodies are members of Christ himself?[919]

Therefore, I urge you, brothers and sisters, in view of God's mercy, to offer your bodies as a living *sacrifice*, holy and pleasing to God—this is your true and proper worship.[920]

Let the name of the LORD be praised, both now and forevermore.[921]

Through Jesus, therefore, let us continually offer to God a *sacrifice* of praise—the fruit of lips that openly confess his name.[922]

Command them to do good, to be rich in good deeds, and to be generous and willing to share.[923]

And do not forget to do good and to share with others, for with such *sacrifice*s God is pleased.[924]

Salvation

The wrath of God is being revealed from heaven against all the godlessness and wickedness of people, who suppress the truth by their wickedness,[925]

For God did not appoint us to suffer wrath but to receive *salvation* through our Lord Jesus Christ.[926]

Our God is a God who saves; from the Sovereign LORD comes escape from death.[927]

how shall we escape if we ignore such a great salvation? This *salvation,* which was first announced by the Lord, was confirmed to us by those who heard him.[928]

He chose to give us birth through the word of truth, that we might be a kind of firstfruits of all he created.[929]

And you also were included in Christ when you heard the word of truth, the gospel of your *salvation*.[930]

Jesus answered, "I am the way and the truth and the life. No one comes to the Father except through me.[931]

***Salvation* is found in no one else, for there is no other name under heaven given to mankind by which we must be saved."[932]**

And everyone who calls on the name of the Lord will be saved.'[933]

I will lift up the cup of *salvation* and call on the name of the LORD.[934]

All those the Father gives me will come to me, and whoever comes to me I will never drive away.[935]

But I pray to you, LORD, in the time of your favor; in your great love, O God, answer me with your sure *salvation*.[936]

Take my yoke upon you and learn from me, for I am gentle and humble in heart, and you will find rest for your souls.[937]

Truly my soul finds rest in God; my salvation comes from him.[938]

but whoever drinks the water I give them will never thirst. Indeed, the water I give them will become in them a spring of water welling up to eternal life."[939]

With joy you will draw water from the wells of *salvation*.[940]

When Jesus spoke again to the people, he said, "I am the light of the world. Whoever follows me will never walk in darkness, but will have the light of life."[941]

The LORD is my light and my *salvation*— whom shall I fear?[942]

Then the righteous will shine like the sun in the kingdom of their Father. Whoever has ears, let them hear.[943]

The *salvation* of the righteous comes from the LORD; he is their stronghold in time of trouble.[944]

Therefore my heart is glad and my tongue rejoices; my body also will live in hope,[945]

But I trust in your unfailing love; my heart rejoices in your *salvation*.[946]

Sin

There is a way that appears to be right, but in the end it leads to death.[947]

The wages of the righteous is life, but the earnings of the wicked are *sin* and death.[948]

The heart is deceitful above all things and beyond cure. Who can understand it?[949]

If we claim to be without *sin*, we deceive ourselves and the truth is not in us.[950]

Do you see a person wise in their own eyes? There is more hope for a fool than for them.[951]

In their own eyes they flatter themselves too much to detect or hate their *sin*.[952]

Nothing in all creation is hidden from God's sight. Everything is uncovered and laid bare before the eyes of him to whom we must give account.[953]

My eyes are on all their ways; they are not hidden from me, nor is their *sin* concealed from my eyes.[954]

For since the creation of the world God's invisible qualities—his eternal power and divine nature—have been clearly seen, being understood from what has been made, so that people are without excuse.[955]

If I had not come and spoken to them, they would not be guilty of *sin*; but now they have no excuse for their *sin*.956

Thanks be to God for his indescribable gift!957

For the wages of *sin* is death, but the gift of God is eternal life in Christ Jesus our Lord.958

God presented Christ as a sacrifice of atonement, through the shedding of his blood—to be received by faith.959

God made him who had no *sin* to be *sin* for us, so that in him we might become the righteousness of God.960

So if the Son sets you free, you will be free indeed.961

Jesus replied, "Very truly I tell you, everyone who *sin*s is a slave to *sin*.962

Then Jesus was led by the Spirit into the wilderness to be tempted by the devil.963

For we do not have a high priest who is unable to empathize with our weaknesses, but we have one who has been tempted in every way, just as we are—yet he did not *sin*.964

Search me, God, and know my heart; test me and know my anxious thoughts.965

Tremble and do not *sin*; when you are on your beds, search your hearts and be silent.[966]

I desire to do your will, my God; your law is within my heart.[967]

I have hidden your word in my heart that I might not *sin* against you.[968]

But from now on, the Son of Man will be seated at the right hand of the mighty God."[969]

My dear children, I write this to you so that you will not *sin*. But if anybody does *sin*, we have an advocate with the Father—Jesus Christ, the Righteous One.[970]

Spirit

For this God is our God for ever and ever; he will be our guide even to the end.[971]

And I will ask the Father, and he will give you another advocate to help you and be with you forever—the *Spirit* of truth. The world cannot accept him, because it neither sees him nor knows him. But you know him, for he lives with you and will be in you.[972]

I will instruct you and teach you in the way you should go; I will counsel you with my loving eye on you.[973]

But the Advocate, the Holy *Spirit*, whom the Father will send in my name, will teach you all things and will remind you of everything I have said to you.[974]

Sanctify them by the truth; your word is truth.[975]

But when he, the *Spirit* of truth, comes, he will guide you into all the truth.[976]

See what great love the Father has lavished on us, that we should be called children of God![977]

For those who are led by the *Spirit* of God are the children of God.[978]

My soul is weary with sorrow; strengthen me according to your word.[979]

I pray that out of his glorious riches he may strengthen you with power through his *Spirit* in your inner being,[980]

I came to you in weakness with great fear and trembling.[981]

In the same way, the *Spirit* helps us in our weakness. We do not know what we ought to pray for, but the *Spirit* himself intercedes for us through wordless groans.[982]

"For my thoughts are not your thoughts, neither are your ways my ways," declares the Lord.[983]

The *Spirit* searches all things, even the deep things of God. For who knows a person's thoughts except their own *spirit* within them? In the same way no one knows the thoughts of God except the *Spirit* of God.[984]

"If I testify about myself, my testimony is not true. There is another who testifies in my favor, and I know that his testimony about me is true.[985]

"When the Advocate comes, whom I will send to you from the Father—the *Spirit* of truth who goes out from the Father—he will testify about me.[986]

Yet to all who did receive him, to those who believed in his name, he gave the right to become children of God—[987]

The *Spirit* himself testifies with our *spirit* that we are God's children.[988]

For in Christ Jesus neither circumcision nor uncircumcision has any value. The only thing that counts is faith expressing itself through love.[989]

As the body without the *spirit* is dead, so faith without deeds is dead.[990]

He guides the humble in what is right and teaches them his way.[991]

Rather, it should be that of your inner self, the unfading beauty of a gentle and quiet *spirit*, which is of great worth in God's sight.[992]

Therefore, since we are receiving a kingdom that cannot be shaken, let us be thankful, and so worship God acceptably with reverence and awe, for our "God is a consuming fire."[993]

Do not quench the *Spirit*.[994]

Thanks

Our God is in heaven; he does whatever pleases him.[995]

Give *thanks* to the God of heaven. His love endures forever.[996]

For the Lord your God is God of gods and Lord of lords, the great God, mighty and awesome, who shows no partiality and accepts no bribes.[997]

Give *thanks* to the God of gods. His love endures forever.[998]

The Lord is good to those whose hope is in him, to the one who seeks him;[999]

Give *thanks* to the LORD, for he is good; his love endures forever.[1000]

The Lord knows all human plans; he knows that they are futile.[1001]

For although they knew God, they neither glorified him as God nor gave *thanks* to him, but their thinking became futile and their foolish hearts were darkened.[1002]

For the wages of sin is death, but the gift of God is eternal life in Christ Jesus our Lord.[1003]

***Thanks* be to God for his indescribable gift![1004]**

When the perishable has been clothed with the imperishable, and the mortal with immortality, then the saying that is written will come true: "Death has been swallowed up in victory."[1005]

But *thanks* be to God! He gives us the victory through our Lord Jesus Christ.[1006]

And everyone who calls on the name of the Lord will be saved.'[1007]

I will give you *thanks*, for you answered me; you have become my salvation.[1008]

"Enter through the narrow gate. For wide is the gate and broad is the road that leads to destruction, and many enter through it."[1009]

Open for me the gates of the righteous; I will enter and give *thanks* to the Lord.[1010]

Every good and perfect gift is from above, coming down from the Father of the heavenly lights, who does not change like shifting shadows.[1011]

Sing and make music from your heart to the Lord, always giving *thanks* to God the Father for everything, in the name of our Lord Jesus Christ.[1012]

May these words of my mouth and this meditation of my heart be pleasing in your sight, Lord, my Rock and my Redeemer.[1013]

And whatever you do, whether in word or deed, do it all in the name of the Lord Jesus, giving *thanks* to God the Father through him.[1014]

I will extol the Lord at all times; his praise will always be on my lips.[1015]

Rejoice always, pray continually, give *thanks* in all circumstances; for this is God's will for you in Christ Jesus.[1016]

The Lord reigns, he is robed in majesty; the Lord is robed in majesty and armed with strength; indeed, the world is established, firm and secure.[1017]

And the twenty-four elders, who were seated on their thrones before God, fell on their faces and worshiped God, saying: "We give *thanks* to you, Lord God Almighty, the One who is and who was, because you have taken your great power and have begun to reign.[1018]

Water

"Who shut up the sea behind doors when it burst forth from the womb, when I made the clouds its garment and wrapped it in thick darkness, when I fixed limits for it and set its doors and bars in place, when I said, 'This far you may come and no farther; here is where your proud waves halt'?[1019]

And God said, "Let the *water* under the sky be gathered to one place, and let dry ground appear." And it was so.[1020]

People were eating, drinking, marrying and being given in marriage up to the day Noah entered the ark. Then the flood came and destroyed them all.[1021]

The *water*s rose and increased greatly on the earth, and the ark floated on the surface of the *water*.[1022]

Isaac brought her into the tent of his mother Sarah, and he married Rebekah.[1023]

May it be that when I say to a young woman, 'Please let down your jar that I may have a drink,' and she says, 'Drink, and I'll *water* your camels too'—let her be the one you have chosen for your servant Isaac.[1024]

By faith Moses' parents hid him for three months after he was born, because they saw he was no ordinary child, and they were not afraid of the king's edict.[1025]

When the child grew older, she took him to Pharaoh's daughter and he became her son. She named him Moses, saying, "I drew him out of the *water*."[1026]

By faith the people passed through the Red Sea as on dry land; but when the Egyptians tried to do so, they were drowned.[1027]

Raise your staff and stretch out your hand over the sea to divide the *water* so that the Israelites can go through the sea on dry ground.[1028]

The LORD himself goes before you and will be with you; he will never leave you nor forsake you.[1029]

I will stand there before you by the rock at Horeb. Strike the rock, and *water* will come out of it for the people to drink."[1030]

You are the God who performs miracles; you display your power among the peoples.[1031]

and the master of the banquet tasted the *water* that had been turned into wine.[1032]

Believe me when I say that I am in the Father and the Father is in me; or at least believe on the evidence of the works themselves.[1033]

When they had rowed about three or four miles, they saw Jesus approaching the boat, walking on the *water*; and they were frightened.[1034]

And he is the head of the body, the church; he is the beginning and the firstborn from among the dead, so that in everything he might have the supremacy.[1035]

Husbands, love your wives, just as Christ loved the church and gave himself up for her to make her holy, cleansing her by the washing with *water* through the word, and to present her to himself as a radiant church, without stain or wrinkle or any other blemish, but holy and blameless.[1036]

For then there will be great distress, unequaled from the beginning of the world until now—and never to be equaled again.[1037]

The third angel poured out his bowl on the rivers and springs of *water*, and they became blood.[1038]

There is a river whose streams make glad the city of God, the holy place where the Most High dwells.[1039]

Then the angel showed me the river of the *water* of life, as clear as crystal, flowing from the throne of God and of the Lamb down the middle of the great street of the city.[1040]

But if from there you seek the Lord your God, you will find him if you seek him with all your heart and with all your soul.[1041]

As the deer pants for streams of *water*, so my soul pants for you, my God.[1042]

Wisdom

The heavens are yours, and yours also the earth; you founded the world and all that is in it.[1043]

But God made the earth by his power; he founded the world by his *wisdom* and stretched out the heavens by his understanding.[1044]

How great are your works, LORD, how profound your thoughts![1045]

His *wisdom* is profound, his power is vast. Who has resisted him and come out unscathed?[1046]

He is the Lord our God; his judgments are in all the earth.[1047]

Oh, the depth of the riches of the *wisdom* and knowledge of God! How unsearchable his judgments, and his paths beyond tracing out![1048]

The Spirit searches all things, even the deep things of God.[1049]

This is what we speak, not in words taught us by human *wisdom* but in words taught by the Spirit, explaining spiritual realities with Spirit-taught words.[1050]

A good person leaves an inheritance for their children's children, but a sinner's wealth is stored up for the righteous.[1051]

***Wisdom*, like an inheritance, is a good thing and benefits those who see the sun.[1052]**

This is what the Lord Almighty says: "Give careful thought to your ways."[1053]

The *wisdom* of the prudent is to give thought to their ways, but the folly of fools is deception.[1054]

Do not be wise in your own eyes; fear the LORD and shun evil.[1055]

And he said to the human race, "The fear of the Lord—that is *wisdom*, and to shun evil is understanding."[1056]

But the plans of the Lord stand firm forever, the purposes of his heart through all generations.[1057]

All this also comes from the Lord Almighty, whose plan is wonderful, whose *wisdom* is magnificent.[1058]

May these words of my mouth and this meditation of my heart be pleasing in your sight, Lord, my Rock and my Redeemer.[1059]

My mouth will speak words of *wisdom*; the meditation of my heart will give you understanding.[1060]

Gold there is, and rubies in abundance, but lips that speak knowledge are a rare jewel.[1061]

Coral and jasper are not worthy of mention; the price of *wisdom* is beyond rubies.[1062]

A good man brings good things out of the good stored up in his heart, and an evil man brings evil things out of the evil stored up in his heart. For the mouth speaks what the heart is full of.[1063]

The mouths of the righteous utters *wisdom*, and their tongues speak what is just.[1064]

Ask and it will be given to you; seek and you will find; knock and the door will be opened to you.[1065]

If any of you lacks *wisdom*, you should ask God, who gives generously to all without finding fault, and it will be given to you.[1066]

Word

I and the Father are one."[1067]

The Son is the radiance of God's glory and the exact representation of his being, sustaining all things by his powerful *word*.[1068]

Through him all things were made; without him nothing was made that has been made.[1069]

By the *word* of the Lord the heavens were made, their starry host by the breath of his mouth.[1070]

For truly I tell you, until heaven and earth disappear, not the smallest letter, not the least stroke of a pen, will by any means disappear from the Law until everything is accomplished.[1071]

The grass withers and the flowers fall, but the *word* of our God stands forever."[1072]

So God created mankind in his own image, in the image of God he created them; male and female he created them.[1073]

He chose to give us birth through the *word* of truth, that we might be a kind of firstfruits of all he created.[1074]

All of us have become like one who is unclean, and all our righteous acts are like filthy rags; we all shrivel up like a leaf, and like the wind our sins sweep us away.[1075]

If we claim we have not sinned, we make him out to be a liar and his *word* is not in us.[1076]

"The virgin will conceive and give birth to a son, and they will call him Immanuel" (which means "God with us").[1077]

The *Word* became flesh and made his dwelling among us. We have seen his glory, the glory of the one and only Son, who came from the Father, full of grace and truth.[1078]

For God so loved the world that he gave his one and only Son, that whoever believes in him shall not perish but have eternal life.[1079]

He sent out his *word* and healed them; he rescued them from the grave.[1080]

My eyes are on all their ways; they are not hidden from me, nor is their sin concealed from my eyes.[1081]

I have hidden your *word* in my heart that I might not sin against you.[1082]

All Scripture is God-breathed and is useful for teaching, rebuking, correcting and training in righteousness, so that the servant of God may be thoroughly equipped for every good work.[1083]

Every *word* of God is flawless; he is a shield to those who take refuge in him.[1084]

Search me, God, and know my heart; test me and know my anxious thoughts.[1085]

For the *word* of God is alive and active. Sharper than any double-edged sword, it penetrates even to dividing soul and spirit, joints and marrow; it judges the thoughts and attitudes of the heart.[1086]

Therefore, there is now no condemnation for those who are in Christ Jesus, because through Christ Jesus the law of the Spirit who gives life has set you free from the law of sin and death.[1087]

"Very truly I tell you, whoever hears my *word* and believes him who sent me has eternal life and will not be judged but has crossed over from death to life.[1088]

Worship

Do you not know? Have you not heard? The Lord is the everlasting God, the Creator of the ends of the earth.[1089]

Worship him who made the heavens, the earth, the sea and the springs of waters!"[1090]

But when he, the Spirit of truth, comes, he will guide you into all the truth.[1091]

God is spirit, and his worshipers must worship in the spirit and in truth."[1092]

It is written: "'As surely as I live,' says the Lord, 'every knee will bow before me; every tongue will acknowledge God.'"[1093]

Come, let us bow down in worship, let us kneel before the Lord our Maker; for he is our God and we are the people of his pasture, the flock under his care.[1094]

Our Redeemer—the Lord Almighty is his name— is the Holy One of Israel.[1095]

Ascribe to the Lord the glory due his name; worship the Lord in the splendor of holiness.[1096]

In the beginning was the Word, and the Word was with God, and the Word was God.[1097]

And again, when God brings his firstborn into the world, he says "Let all God's angels worship him."[1098]

"You are a king, then!" said Pilate. Jesus answered, "You say that I am a king. In fact, the reason I was born and came into the world is to testify to the truth.[1099]

After Jesus was born in Bethlehem in Judea, during the time of King Herod, Magi from the east came to Jerusalem and asked, "Where is the one who has been born king of the Jews? We saw his star when it rose and have come to *worship* him."[1100]

Therefore the Lord himself will give you a sign: The virgin will conceive and give birth to a son, and will call him Immanuel.[1101]

On coming to the house, they saw the child with his mother Mary, and they bowed down and *worship*ed him.[1102]

All a person's ways seem pure to them, but motives are weighed by the Lord.[1103]

They *worship* me in vain; their teachings are merely human rules.'"[1104]

All his days the wicked man suffers torment, the ruthless man through all the years stored up for him.[1105]

And the smoke of their torment will rise for ever and ever. There will be no rest day or night for those who *worship* the beast and its image, or for anyone who receives the mark of its name."[1106]

"You shall not make for yourself an image in the form of anything in heaven above or on the earth beneath or in the waters below.[1107]

Worship God!"[1108]

As you come to him, the living Stone—rejected by humans but chosen by God and precious to him—you also, like living stones, are being built into a spiritual house to be a holy priesthood, offering spiritual sacrifices acceptable to God through Jesus Christ.[1109]

Therefore, I urge you, brothers and sisters, in view of God's mercy, to offer your bodies as a living sacrifice, holy and pleasing to God—this is your true and proper worship.[1110]

TWO

A selection of scripture readings based on word subjects from the Book of Proverbs

Proverbs 30:5 New International Version (NIV)

"Every word of God is flawless; he is a shield to those who take refuge in him.

Evil

And we know that in all things God works for the good of those who love him, who have been called according to his purpose.[1111]

Through love and faithfulness sin is atoned for; through the fear of the Lord *evil* is avoided.[1112]

Will you keep to the old path that the wicked have trod?[1113]

Do not set foot on the path of the wicked or walk in the way of *evil*doers.[1114]

"I am unworthy—how can I reply to you? I put my hand over my mouth.[1115]

"If you play the fool and exalt yourself, or if you plan *evil*, clap your hand over your mouth![1116]

Woe to those who are wise in their own eyes and clever in their own sight.[1117]

Do not be wise in your own eyes; fear the Lord and shun *evil*.[1118]

"If anyone causes one of these little ones—those who believe in me—to stumble, it would be better for them to have a large millstone hung around their neck and to be drowned in the depths of the sea.[1119]

Whoever leads the upright along an *evil* path will fall into their own trap, but the blameless will receive a good inheritance.[1120]

Learn to do right; seek justice. Defend the oppressed. Take up the cause of the fatherless; plead the case of the widow.[1121]

Evildoers do not understand what is right, but those who seek the Lord understand it fully.[1122]

So be careful to do what the Lord your God has commanded you; do not turn aside to the right or to the left.[1123]

Do not turn to the right or the left; keep your foot from *evil*.[1124]

See, I set before you today life and prosperity, death and destruction.[1125]

Truly the righteous attain life, but whoever pursues *evil* finds death.[1126]

Pharaoh said, "Who is the Lord, that I should obey him and let Israel go? I do not know the Lord and I will not let Israel go."[1127]

The *evil* deeds of the wicked ensnare them; the cords of their sins hold them fast.[1128]

Again his Jewish opponents picked up stones to stone him, but Jesus said to them, "I have shown you many good works from the Father. For which of these do you stone me?"[1129]

Evil will never leave the house of one who pays back *evil* for good.[1130]

Therefore God exalted him to the highest place and gave him the name that is above every name, that at the name of Jesus every knee should bow, in heaven and on earth and under the earth, and every tongue acknowledge that Jesus Christ is Lord, to the glory of God the Father.[1131]

Evildoers will bow down in the presence of the good, and the wicked at the gates of the righteous.[1132]

Fool

Who is wise? Let them realize these things. Who is discerning? Let them understand. The ways of the Lord are right; the righteous walk in them, but the rebellious stumble in them.[1133]

The way of *fool*s seems right to them, but the wise listen to advice.[1134]

This is what the Lord says: "Cursed is the one who trusts in man, who draws strength from mere flesh and whose heart turns away from the Lord.[1135]

Those who trust in themselves are *fool*s, but those who walk in wisdom are kept safe.[1136]

Be very careful, then, how you live—not as unwise but as wise, making the most of every opportunity, because the days are evil.[1137]

All who are prudent act with knowledge, but *fool*s expose their folly.[1138]

Whoever obeys his command will come to no harm, and the wise heart will know the proper time and procedure.[1139]

The wise in heart accept commands, but a chattering *fool* comes to ruin.[1140]

Do not let those gloat over me who are my enemies without cause; do not let those who hate me without reason maliciously wink the eye.[1141]

Whoever winks maliciously causes grief, and a chattering *fool* comes to ruin.[1142]

If only you would be altogether silent! For you, that would be wisdom.[1143]

Even *fool*s are thought wise if they keep silent, and discerning if they hold their tongues.[1144]

My dear brothers and sisters, take note of this: Everyone should be quick to listen, slow to speak and slow to become angry, because human anger does not produce the righteousness that God desires.[1145]

***Fool*s give full vent to their rage, but the wise bring calm in the end.**[1146]

Those whom I love I rebuke and discipline. So be earnest and repent.[1147]

A rebuke impresses a discerning person more than a hundred lashes a *fool*.[1148]

You, Lord, will keep the needy safe and will protect us forever from the wicked, who freely strut about when what is vile is honored by the human race.[1149]

Like snow in summer or rain in harvest, honor is not fitting for a *fool*.[1150]

Don't have anything to do with foolish and stupid arguments, because you know they produce quarrels.[1151]

It is to one's honor to avoid strife, but every *fool* is quick to quarrel.[1152]

But when Pharaoh saw that there was relief, he hardened his heart and would not listen to Moses and Aaron, just as the Lord had said.[1153]

As a dog returns to its vomit, so *fools* repeat their folly.[1154]

Then Nebuchadnezzar was furious with Shadrach, Meshach and Abednego, and his attitude toward them changed. He ordered the furnace heated seven times hotter than usual[1155]

Stone is heavy and sand a burden, but a *fool*'s provocation is heavier than both.[1156]

Good

"His eyes are on the ways of mortals; he sees their every step.[1157]

The eyes of the Lord are everywhere, keeping watch on the wicked and the *good*.[1158]

But the angel said to them, "Do not be afraid. I bring you good news that will cause great joy for all the people.[1159]

Light in a messenger's eyes brings joy to the heart, and *good* news gives health to the bones.[1160]

But which of them has stood in the council of the Lord to see or to hear his word? Who has listened and heard his word?[1161]

Thus you will walk in the ways of the *good* and keep to the paths of the righteous.[1162]

The secret things belong to the Lord our God, but the things revealed belong to us and to our children forever, that we may follow all the words of this law.[1163]

It is not *good* to eat too much honey, nor is it honorable to search out matters that are too deep.[1164]

How sweet are your words to my taste, sweeter than honey to my mouth![1165]

Eat honey, my son, for it is *good*; honey from the comb is sweet to your taste.[1166]

I will declare your name to my people; in the assembly I will praise you.[1167]

Then you will find favor and a *good* name in the sight of God and man.[1168]

Your words have supported those who stumbled; you have strengthened faltering knees.[1169]

A person finds joy in giving an apt reply—and how *good* is a timely word![1170]

It cannot be bought with the finest gold, nor can its price be weighed out in silver.[1171]

A *good* name is more desirable than great riches; to be esteemed is better than silver or gold.[1172]

The wicked band together against the righteous and condemn the innocent to death.[1173]

It is not *good* to be partial to the wicked and so deprive the innocent of justice.[1174]

Tell the righteous it will be well with them, for they will enjoy the fruit of their deeds.[1175]

From the fruit of their lips people are filled with *good* things, and the work of their hands brings them reward.[1176]

For we must all appear before the judgment seat of Christ, so that each of us may receive what is due us for the things done while in the body, whether good or bad.[1177]

The faithless will be fully repaid for their ways, and the *good* rewarded for theirs.[1178]

Give to everyone what you owe them: If you owe taxes, pay taxes; if revenue, then revenue; if respect, then respect; if honor, then honor.[1179]

Do not withhold *good* from those to whom it is due, when it is in your power to act.[1180]

Righteous and Wicked

Who is going to harm you if you are eager to do good?[1181]

No harm overtakes the *righteous*, but the *wicked* have their fill of *trouble*.[1182]

If I had cherished sin in my heart, the Lord would not have listened; but God has surely listened and has heard my prayer.[1183]

The Lord is far from the *wicked*, but he hears the prayer of the *righteous*.[1184]

You adulterous people, don't you know that friendship with the world means enmity against God? Therefore, anyone who chooses to be a friend of the world becomes an enemy of God.[1185]

The *righteous* choose their friends carefully, but the way of the *wicked* leads them astray.[1186]

Woe to those who make unjust laws, to those who issue oppressive decrees, to deprive the poor of their rights and withhold justice from the oppressed of my people, making widows their prey and robbing the fatherless.[1187]

The *righteous* care about justice for the poor, but the *wicked* have no such concern.[1188]

Do not lie to each other, since you have taken off your old self with its practices and have put on the new self, which is being renewed in knowledge in the image of its Creator.[1189]

The *righteous* hate what is false, but the *wicked* make themselves a stench and bring shame on themselves.[1190]

"Then the king told the attendants, 'Tie him hand and foot, and throw him outside, into the darkness, where there will be weeping and gnashing of teeth.'[1191]

The light of the *righteous* shines brightly, but the lamp of the *wicked* is snuffed out.[1192]

The memory of him perishes from the earth; he has no name in the land.[1193]

The name of the *righteous* is used in blessings, but the name of the *wicked* will rot.[1194]

'Never again will they hunger; never again will they thirst.[1195]

The Lord does not let the *righteous* go hungry, but he thwarts the craving of the *wicked*.[1196]

But in your hearts revere Christ as Lord. Always be prepared to give an answer to everyone who asks you to give the reason for the hope that you have.[1197]

The heart of the *righteous* weighs its answers, but the mouth of the *wicked* gushes evil.[1198]

Do not be surprised, my brothers and sisters, if the world hates you.[1199]

The *righteous* detest the dishonest; the *wicked* detest the upright.[1200]

The weapons we fight with are not the weapons of the world. On the contrary, they have divine power to demolish strongholds.[1201]

The *wicked* desire the stronghold of evildoers, but the root of the *righteous* endures.[1202]

I will set my face against you so that you will be defeated by your enemies; those who hate you will rule over you, and you will flee even when no one is pursuing you.[1203]

The *wicked* flee though no one pursues, but the *righteous* are as bold as a lion.[1204]

Spirit

With the tongue we praise our Lord and Father, and with it we curse human beings, who have been made in God's likeness.[1205]

The soothing tongue is a tree of life, but a perverse tongue crushes the *spirit*.[1206]

I had not been sad in his presence before, so the king asked me, "Why does your face look so sad when you are not ill? This can be nothing but sadness of heart."[1207]

A happy heart makes the face cheerful, but heartache crushes the *spirit*.[1208]

The eyes of the arrogant will be humbled and human pride brought low; the Lord alone will be exalted in that day.[1209]

Pride goes before destruction, a haughty *spirit* before a fall.[1210]

The Lord sends poverty and wealth; he humbles and he exalts.[1211]

Better to be lowly in *spirit* along with the oppressed than to share plunder with the proud.[1212]

Then he said to me: "Son of man, these bones are the people of Israel. They say, 'Our bones are dried up and our hope is gone; we are cut off.'[1213]

A cheerful heart is good medicine, but a crushed *spirit* dries up the bones.[1214]

For I am poor and needy, and my heart is wounded within me.[1215]

The human *spirit* can endure in sickness, but a crushed *spirit* who can bear?[1216]

You, Lord, are my lamp; the Lord turns my darkness into light.[1217]

The human *spirit* is the lamp of the Lord that sheds light on one's inmost being.[1218]

For those who exalt themselves will be humbled, and those who humble themselves will be exalted.[1219]

Pride brings a person low, but the lowly in *spirit* gain honor.[1220]

It is God's will that you should be sanctified: that you should avoid sexual immorality; that each of you should learn to control your own body in a way that is holy and honorable, not in passionate lust like the pagans, who do not know God;[1221]

Surely her house leads down to death and her paths to the *spirit*s of the dead.[1222]

There was a man sent from God whose name was John.[1223]

Like a snow-cooled drink at harvest time is a trustworthy messenger to the one who sends him; he refreshes the *spirit* of his master.[1224]

Upright

Now this is our boast: Our conscience testifies that we have conducted ourselves in the world, and especially in our relations with you, with integrity and godly sincerity. We have done so, relying not on worldly wisdom but on God's grace.[1225]

He holds success in store for the *upright*, he is a shield to those whose walk is blameless,[1226]

The righteous will inherit the land and dwell in it forever.[1227]

For the *upright* will live in the land, and the blameless will remain in it;[1228]

Anyone who chooses to do the will of God will find out whether my teaching comes from God or whether I speak on my own.[1229]

For the Lord detests the perverse but takes the *upright* into his confidence.[1230]

Should not your piety be your confidence and your blameless ways your hope?[1231]

The integrity of the *upright* guides them, but the unfaithful are destroyed by their duplicity.[1232]

For by your words you will be acquitted, and by your words you will be condemned."[1233]

The words of the wicked lie in wait for blood, but the speech of the *upright* rescues them.[1234]

Then Peter came to Jesus and asked, "Lord, how many times shall I forgive my brother or sister who sins against me? Up to seven times?" Jesus answered, "I tell you, not seven times, but seventy-seven times.[1235]

Fools mock at making amends for sin, but goodwill is found among the *upright*.[1236]

For we know that if the earthly tent we live in is destroyed, we have a building from God, an eternal house in heaven, not built by human hands.[1237]

The house of the wicked will be destroyed, but the tent of the *upright* will flourish.[1238]

For the eyes of the Lord are on the righteous and his ears are attentive to their prayer, but the face of the Lord is against those who do evil."[1239]

The Lord detests the sacrifice of the wicked, but the prayer of the *upright* pleases him.[1240]

Turn from evil and do good; then you will dwell in the land forever.[1241]

The highway of the *upright* avoids evil; those who guard their ways preserve their lives.[1242]

While they were stoning him, Stephen prayed, "Lord Jesus, receive my spirit."[1243]

The bloodthirsty hate a person of integrity and seek to kill the _upright_.[1244]

Yet having learned who Mordecai's people were, he scorned the idea of killing only Mordecai. Instead Haman looked for a way to destroy all Mordecai's people, the Jews, throughout the whole kingdom of Xerxes.[1245]

Whoever fears the Lord walks _upright_ly, but those who despise him are devious in their ways.[1246]

Through these he has given us his very great and precious promises, so that through them you may participate in the divine nature, having escaped the corruption in the world caused by evil desires.[1247]

The righteousness of the _upright_ delivers them, but the unfaithful are trapped by evil desires.[1248]

Wisdom and Understanding

Through him all things were made; without him nothing was made that has been made.[1249]

By *wisdom* the Lord laid the earth's foundations, by *understanding* he set the heavens in place;[1250]

It cannot be bought with the finest gold, nor can its price be weighed out in silver.[1251]

Blessed are those who find *wisdom*, those who gain *understanding*,[1252]

Accept instruction from his mouth and lay up his words in your heart.[1253]

For the Lord gives *wisdom*; from his mouth come knowledge and *understanding*.[1254]

Jesus answered, "It is written: 'Man shall not live on bread alone, but on every word that comes from the mouth of God.'"[1255]

Get *wisdom*, get *understanding*; do not forget my words or turn away from them.[1256]

Blessed is the one who does not walk in step with the wicked or stand in the way that sinners take or sit in the company of mockers, but whose delight is in the law of the Lord, and who meditates on his law day and night.[1257]

A fool finds pleasure in wicked schemes, but a person of *understanding* delights in *wisdom*.[1258]

As Jesus was saying these things, a woman in the crowd called out, "Blessed is the mother who gave you birth and nursed you."[1259]

Does not *wisdom* call out? Does not *understanding* raise her voice?[1260]

"The kingdom of heaven is like treasure hidden in a field. When a man found it, he hid it again, and then in his joy went and sold all he had and bought that field.[1261]

The beginning of *wisdom* is this: Get *wisdom*. Though it cost all you have, get *understanding*.[1262]

For I know the plans I have for you," declares the Lord, "plans to prosper you and not to harm you, plans to give you hope and a future.[1263]

The one who gets *wisdom* loves life; the one who cherishes *understanding* will soon prosper.[1264]

Moses listened to his father-in-law and did everything he said. He chose capable men from all Israel and made them leaders of the people, officials over thousands, hundreds, fifties and tens. They served as judges for the people at all times.[1265]

My son, do not let *wisdom* and *understanding* out of your sight, preserve sound judgment and discretion;[1266]

For we are co-workers in God's service; you are God's field, God's building.[1267]

By *wisdom* a house is built, and through *understanding* it is established;[1268]

Now all has been heard; here is the conclusion of the matter: Fear God and keep his commandments, for this is the duty of all mankind.[1269]

The fear of the Lord is the beginning of *wisdom*, and knowledge of the Holy One is *understanding*.[1270]

THREE

A selection of scriptural readings based on the Book of Psalms

Psalm 119:89 New International Version (NIV)

Your word, Lord, is eternal; it stands firm in the heavens.

Psalm 1

Blessed is the one who does not walk in step with the wicked[1271]

Do not set foot on the path of the wicked or walk in the way of evildoers.[1272]

or stand in the way that sinners take[1273]

There is a way that appears to be right, but in the end it leads to death.[1274]

or sit in the company of mockers,[1275]

Surely mockers surround me; my eyes must dwell on their hostility.[1276]

but whose delight is in the law of the Lord,[1277]

For in my inner being I delight in God's law;[1278]

and who meditates on his law day and night.[1279]

Oh, how I love your law! I meditate on it all day long.[1280]

That person is like a tree planted by streams of water,[1281]

They will be like a tree planted by the water that sends out its roots by the stream.[1282]

which yields its fruit in season and whose leaf does not wither—1283

In times of disaster they will not wither; in days of famine they will enjoy plenty.[1284]

whatever they do prospers.[1285]

For I know the plans I have for you," declares the Lord, "plans to prosper you and not to harm you, plans to give you hope and a future.[1286]

Not so the wicked! They are like chaff that the wind blows away.[1287]

On the wicked he will rain fiery coals and burning sulfur; a scorching wind will be their lot.[1288]

Therefore the wicked will not stand in the judgment,[1289]

For we must all appear before the judgment seat of Christ, so that each of us may receive what is due us for the things done while in the body, whether good or bad.[1290]

nor sinners in the assembly of the righteous.[1291]

In Hades, where he was in torment, he looked up and saw Abraham far away, with Lazarus by his side.[1292]

For the Lord watches over the way of the righteous,[1293]

Surely, Lord, you bless the righteous; you surround them with your favor as with a shield.[1294]

but the way of the wicked leads to destruction.[1295]

But all sinners will be destroyed; there will be no future for the wicked.[1296]

Psalm 8

Lord, our Lord, how majestic is your name in all the earth![1297]

Therefore God exalted him to the highest place and gave him the name that is above every name, that at the name of Jesus every knee should bow, in heaven and on earth and under the earth,[1298]

You have set your glory in the heavens.[1299]

Therefore, since we have a great high priest who has ascended into heaven, Jesus the Son of God, let us hold firmly to the faith we profess.[1300]

Through the praise of children and infants you have established a stronghold against your enemies, to silence the foe and the avenger.[1301]

"Do you hear what these children are saying?" they asked him. "Yes," replied Jesus, "have you never read, "'From the lips of children and infants you, Lord, have called forth your praise'?"[1302]

When I consider your heavens, the work of your fingers, the moon and the stars, which you have set in place,[1303]

Do you not know? Have you not heard? The Lord is the everlasting God, the Creator of the ends of the earth.[1304]

what is mankind that you are mindful of them, human beings that you care for them?[1305]

For God so loved the world that he gave his one and only Son, that whoever believes in him shall not perish but have eternal life.[1306]

You have made them a little lower than the angels and crowned them with glory and honor.[1307]

So God created mankind in his own image, in the image of God he created them; male and female he created them.[1308]

You made them rulers over the works of your hands; you put everything under their feet:[1309]

God blessed them and said to them, "Be fruitful and increase in number; fill the earth and subdue it.[1310]

all flocks and herds, and the animals of the wild,[1311]

the birds in the sky, and the fish in the sea, all that swim the paths of the seas.[1312]

Then God said, "Let us make mankind in our image, in our likeness, so that they may rule over the fish in the sea and the birds in the sky, over the livestock and all the wild animals, and over all the creatures that move along the ground."[1313]

Lord, our Lord, how majestic is your name in all the earth![1314]

To him who is able to keep you from stumbling and to present you before his glorious presence without fault and with great joy—to the only God our Savior be glory, majesty, power and authority, through Jesus Christ our Lord, before all ages, now and forevermore! Amen.[1315]

Psalm 14

The fool says in his heart, "There is no God."[1316]

The god of this age has blinded the minds of unbelievers, so that they cannot see the light of the gospel that displays the glory of Christ, who is the image of God.[1317]

They are corrupt, their deeds are vile; there is no one who does good.[1318]

This is the verdict: Light has come into the world, but people loved darkness instead of light because their deeds were evil.[1319]

The Lord looks down from heaven on all mankind [1320]

After Jesus said this, he looked toward heaven and prayed: "Father, the hour has come. Glorify your Son, that your Son may glorify you.[1321]

to see if there are any who understand,[1322]

We know also that the Son of God has come and has given us understanding, so that we may know him who is true.[1323]

any who seek God.[1324]

For the Son of man came to seek and to save the lost."[1325]

All have turned away, all have become corrupt;[1326]

But God demonstrates his own love for us in this: While we were still sinners, Christ died for us.[1327]

there is no one who does good, not even one.[1328]

God made him who had no sin to be sin for us, so that in him we might become the righteousness of God.[1329]

Do all these evildoers know nothing?[1330]

Jesus then left that place and went into the region of Judea and across the Jordan. Again crowds of people came to him, and as was his custom, he taught them.[1331]

They devour my people as though eating bread; they never call on the Lord.[1332]

And everyone who calls on the name of the Lord will be saved.'[1333]

But there they are, overwhelmed with dread,[1334]

Therefore, there is now no condemnation for those who are in Christ Jesus,[1335]

for God is present in the company of the righteous.[1336]

While Jesus was having dinner at Matthew's house, many tax collectors and sinners came and ate with him and his disciples.[1337]

You evildoers frustrate the plans of the poor,[1338]

remember this: Whoever turns a sinner from the error of their way will save them from death and cover over a multitude of sins.[1339]

but the Lord is their refuge.[1340]

Come to me, all you who are weary and burdened, and I will give you rest.[1341]

Oh, that salvation for Israel would come out of Zion![1342]

"From this man's descendants God has brought to Israel the Savior Jesus, as he promised.[1343]

When the Lord restores his people, let Jacob rejoice and Israel be glad![1344]

And the God of all grace, who called you to his eternal glory in Christ, after you have suffered a little while, will himself restore you and make you strong, firm and steadfast.[1345]

Psalm 15

Lord, who may dwell in your sacred tent?[1346]

I pray that out of his glorious riches he may strengthen you with power through his Spirit in your inner being, so that Christ may dwell in your hearts through faith.[1347]

Who may live on your holy mountain?[1348]

 "Woman," Jesus replied, "believe me, a time is coming when you will worship the Father neither on this mountain nor in Jerusalem.[1349]

The one whose walk is blameless,[1350]

For he chose us in him before the creation of the world to be holy and blameless in his sight.[1351]

who does what is righteous,[1352]

This righteousness is given through faith in Jesus Christ to all who believe.[1353]

who speaks the truth from their heart;[1354]

Now that you have purified yourselves by obeying the truth so that you have sincere love for each other, love one another deeply, from the heart.[1355]

whose tongue utters no slander,[1356]

Those who consider themselves religious and yet do not keep a tight rein on their tongues deceive themselves, and their religion is worthless.[1357]

who does no wrong to a neighbor,[1358]

Each of us should please our neighbors for their good, to build them up.[1359]

and casts no slur on others;[1360]

Brothers and sisters, do not slander one another.[1361]

who despises a vile person[1362]

Hate what is evil; cling to what is good.[1363]

but honors those who fear the Lord;[1364]

This is how we know what love is: Jesus Christ laid down his life for us. And we ought to lay down our lives for our brothers and sisters.[1365]

who keeps an oath even when it hurts,[1366]

Do not lie to each other, since you have taken off your old self with its practices and have put on the new self, which is being renewed in knowledge in the image of its Creator.[1367]

and does not change their mind;[1368]

Above all, my brothers and sisters, do not swear—not by heaven or by earth or by anything else. All you need to say is a simple "Yes" or "No." Otherwise you will be condemned.[1369]

who lends money to the poor without interest;[1370]

But now as for what is inside you—be generous to the poor, and everything will be clean for you.[1371]

who does not accept a bribe against the innocent.[1372]

It teaches us to say "No" to ungodliness and worldly passions, and to live self-controlled, upright and godly lives in this present age,[1373]

Whoever does these things will never be shaken.[1374]

Therefore, my dear brothers and sisters, stand firm. Let nothing move you. Always give yourselves fully to the work of the Lord, because you know that your labor in the Lord is not in vain.[1375]

Psalm 19

The heavens declare the glory of God; the skies proclaim the work of his hands.[1376]

Lift up your eyes and look to the heavens: Who created all these? He who brings out the starry host one by one and calls forth each of them by name.[1377]

Day after day they pour forth speech; night after night they reveal knowledge. [1378]

For in him you have been enriched in every way—with all kinds of speech and with all knowledge—[1379]

They have no speech, they use no words; no sound is heard from them. Yet their voice goes out into all the earth, their words to the ends of the world.[1380]

For since the creation of the world God's invisible qualities—his eternal power and divine nature—have been clearly seen, being understood from what has been made, so that people are without excuse.[1381]

In the heavens God has pitched a tent for the sun.[1382]

He stretches out the heavens like a canopy, and spreads them out like a tent to live in.[1383]

It is like a bridegroom coming out of his chamber, like a champion rejoicing to run his course. It rises at one end of the heavens and makes its circuit to the other; nothing is deprived of its warmth.[1384]

The path of the righteous is like the morning sun, shining ever brighter till the full light of day.[1385]

The law of the Lord is perfect, refreshing the soul. The statutes of the Lord are trustworthy, making wise the simple. The precepts of the Lord are right, giving joy to the heart.[1386]

Whoever belongs to God hears what God says.[1387]

The commands of the Lord are radiant, giving light to the eyes.[1388]

Yet I am writing you a new command; its truth is seen in him and in you, because the darkness is passing and the true light is already shining.[1389]

The fear of the Lord is pure, enduring forever.[1390]

He will be the sure foundation for your times, a rich store of salvation and wisdom and knowledge; the fear of the Lord is the key to this treasure.[1391]

The decrees of the Lord are firm, and all of them are righteous. They are more precious than gold, than much pure gold;[1392]

And the words of the Lord are flawless, like silver purified in a crucible, like gold refined seven times.[1393]

they are sweeter than honey, than honey from the honeycomb.[1394]

How sweet are your words to my taste, sweeter than honey to my mouth![1395]

By them your servant is warned; in keeping them there is great reward.[1396]

Whoever believes in the Son has eternal life, but whoever rejects the Son will not see life, for God's wrath remains on them.[1397]

But who can discern their own errors? Forgive my hidden faults.[1398]

"Why do you look at the speck of sawdust in your brother's eye and pay no attention to the plank in your own eye? How can you say to your brother, 'Let me take the speck out of your eye,' when all the time there is a plank in your own eye?[1399]

Keep your servant also from willful sins; may they not rule over me. Then I will be blameless, innocent of great transgression.[1400]

I have hidden your word in my heart that I might not sin against you.[1401]

May these words of my mouth and this meditation of my heart be pleasing in your sight,[1402]

Therefore, I urge you, brothers and sisters, in view of God's mercy, to offer your bodies as a living sacrifice, holy and pleasing to God —this is your true and proper worship.[1403]

Lord, my Rock and my Redeemer.[1404]

I know that my redeemer lives, and that in the end he will stand on the earth.[1405]

Psalm 23

The Lord is my shepherd,[1406]

Now may the God of peace, who through the blood of the eternal covenant brought back from the dead our Lord Jesus, that great Shepherd of the sheep, equip you with everything good for doing his will, and may he work in us what is pleasing to him, through Jesus Christ, to whom be glory for ever and ever. Amen.[1407]

I lack nothing.[1408]

And my God will meet all your needs according to the riches of his glory in Christ Jesus.[1409]

He makes me lie down in green pastures,[1410]

I am the gate; whoever enters through me will be saved. They will come in and go out, and find pasture.[1411]

he leads me beside quiet waters,[1412]

"Come to me, all you who are weary and burdened, and I will give you rest.[1413]

he refreshes my soul.[1414]

May God himself, the God of peace, sanctify you through and through. May your whole spirit, soul and body be kept blameless at the coming of our Lord Jesus Christ.[1415]

He guides me along the right paths for his name's sake.[1416]

You have made known to me the paths of life; you will fill me with joy in your presence.'[1417]

Even though I walk through the darkest valley,[1418]

Then he said to them, "My soul is overwhelmed with sorrow to the point of death. Stay here and keep watch with me."[1419]

I will fear no evil,[1420]

But Jesus immediately said to them: "Take courage! It is I. Don't be afraid."[1421]

for you are with me;[1422]

And surely I am with you always, to the very end of the age."[1423]

your rod and your staff, they comfort me.[1424]

Praise be to the God and Father of our Lord Jesus Christ, the Father of compassion and the God of all comfort, who comforts us in all our troubles, so that we can comfort those in any trouble with the comfort we ourselves receive from God.[1425]

You prepare a table before me in the presence of my enemies.[1426]

Peace I leave with you; my peace I give you. I do not give to you as the world gives.[1427]

You anoint my head with oil;[1428]

you also, like living stones, are being built into a spiritual house to be a holy priesthood, offering spiritual sacrifices acceptable to God through Jesus Christ.[1429]

my cup overflows.[1430]

But the gift is not like the trespass. For if the many died by the trespass of the one man, how much more did God's grace and the gift that came by the grace of the one man, Jesus Christ, overflow to the many![1431]

Surely your goodness and love will follow me all the days of my life,[1432]

being confident of this, that he who began a good work in you will carry it on to completion until the day of Christ Jesus.[1433]

and I will dwell in the house of the Lord forever.[1434]

But our citizenship is in heaven. And we eagerly await a Savior from there, the Lord Jesus Christ,[1435]

Psalm 24

The earth is the Lord's, and everything in it, the world, and all who live in it;[1436]

With all wisdom and understanding, he made known to us the mystery of his will according to his good pleasure, which he purposed in Christ, to be put into effect when the times reach their fulfillment—to bring unity to all things in heaven and on earth under Christ.[1437]

for he founded it on the seas and established it on the waters.[1438]

But they deliberately forget that long ago by God's word the heavens came into being and the earth was formed out of water and by water.[1439]

Who may ascend the mountain of the Lord? Who may stand in his holy place?[1440]

Since, then, you have been raised with Christ, set your hearts on things above, where Christ is, seated at the right hand of God.[1441]

The one who has clean hands and a pure heart, who does not trust in an idol or swear by a false god.[1442]

For it is with your heart that you believe and are justified, and it is with your mouth that you profess your faith and are saved.[1443]

They will receive blessing from the Lord and vindication from God their Savior.[1444]

Praise be to the God and Father of our Lord Jesus Christ, who has blessed us in the heavenly realms with every spiritual blessing in Christ.[1445]

Such is the generation of those who seek him, who seek your face, God of Jacob.[1446]

"Ask and it will be given to you; seek and you will find; knock and the door will be opened to you.[1447]

Lift up your heads, you gates; be lifted up, you ancient doors, that the King of glory may come in.[1448]

I am the gate; whoever enters through me will be saved. They will come in and go out, and find pasture.[1449]

Who is this King of glory? The Lord strong and mighty, the Lord mighty in battle.[1450]

I saw heaven standing open and there before me was a white horse, whose rider is called Faithful and True. With justice he judges and wages war.[1451]

Lift up your heads, you gates; lift them up, you ancient doors, that the King of glory may come in.[1452]

Here I am! I stand at the door and knock. If anyone hears my voice and opens the door, I will come in and eat with that person, and they with me.[1453]

Who is he, this King of glory? The Lord Almighty—he is the King of glory.[1454]

"But what about you?" he asked. "Who do you say I am?" Peter answered, "You are the Messiah."[1455]

Psalm 46

God is our refuge and strength, an ever-present help in trouble.[1456]

"I have told you these things, so that in me you may have peace. In this world you will have trouble. But take heart! I have overcome the world."[1457]

Therefore we will not fear, though the earth give way and the mountains fall into the heart of the sea,[1458]

Every island fled away and the mountains could not be found.[1459]

though its waters roar and foam and the mountains quake with their surging.[1460]

The second angel sounded his trumpet, and something like a huge mountain, all ablaze, was thrown into the sea.[1461]

There is a river whose streams make glad the city of God, the holy place where the Most High dwells.[1462]

Then the angel showed me the river of the water of life, as clear as crystal, flowing from the throne of God and of the Lamb down the middle of the great street of the city.[1463]

God is within her, she will not fall; God will help her at break of day.[1464]

No longer will there be any curse. The throne of God and of the Lamb will be in the city, and his servants will serve him.[1465]

Nations are in uproar, kingdoms fall; he lifts his voice, the earth melts.[1466]

Coming out of his mouth is a sharp sword with which to strike down the nations. "He will rule them with an iron scepter." He treads the winepress of the fury of the wrath of God Almighty.[1467]

The Lord Almighty is with us; the God of Jacob is our fortress.[1468]

The armies of heaven were following him, riding on white horses and dressed in fine linen, white and clean.[1469]

Come and see what the Lord has done, the desolations he has brought on the earth.[1470]

The rest were killed with the sword coming out of the mouth of the rider on the horse, and all the birds gorged themselves on their flesh.[1471]

He makes wars cease to the ends of the earth. He breaks the bow and shatters the spear; He burns the shields with fire.[1472]

He will judge between the nations and will settle disputes for many peoples. They will beat their swords into plowshares and their spears into pruning hooks. Nation will not take up sword against nation, nor will they train for war anymore.[1473]

He says, "Be still, and know that I am God; I will be exalted among the nations, I will be exalted in the earth."[1474]

Therefore God exalted him to the highest place and gave him the name that is above every name, that at the name of Jesus every knee should bow, in heaven and on earth and under the earth,[1475]

The Lord Almighty is with us; the God of Jacob is our fortress.[1476]

And God raised us up with Christ and seated us with him in the heavenly realms in Christ Jesus,[1477]

Psalm 84

How lovely is your dwelling place, Lord Almighty![1478]

Jesus replied, "Foxes have dens and birds have nests, but the Son of Man has no place to lay his head."[1479]

My soul yearns, even faints, for the courts of the Lord; my heart and my flesh cry out for the living God.[1480]

For everyone who asks receives; the one who seeks finds; and to the one who knocks, the door will be opened.[1481]

Even the sparrow has found a home, and the swallow a nest for herself, where she may have her young—a place near your altar, Lord Almighty, my King and my God.[1482]

Are not two sparrows sold for a penny? Yet not one of them will fall to the ground outside your Father's care.[1483]

Blessed are those who dwell in your house; they are ever praising you.[1484]

One of them, when he saw he was healed, came back, praising God in a loud voice.[1485]

Blessed are those whose strength is in you, whose hearts are set on pilgrimage.[1486]

Blessed is anyone who does not stumble on account of me."[1487]

As they pass through the Valley of Baka, they make it a place of springs; the autumn rains also cover it with pools.[1488]

He said to me: "It is done. I am the Alpha and the Omega, the Beginning and the End. To the thirsty I will give water without cost from the spring of the water of life.[1489]

They go from strength to strength, till each appears before God in Zion.[1490]

For we must all appear before the judgment seat of Christ, so that each of us may receive what is due us for the things done while in the body, whether good or bad.[1491]

Hear my prayer, Lord God Almighty; listen to me, God of Jacob.[1492]

While he was still speaking, a bright cloud covered them, and a voice from the cloud said, "This is my Son, whom I love; with him I am well pleased. Listen to him!"[1493]

Look on our shield, O God; look with favor on your anointed one.[1494]

You know what has happened throughout the province of Judea, beginning in Galilee after the baptism that John preached— how God anointed Jesus of Nazareth with the Holy Spirit and power, and how he went around doing good and healing all who were under the power of the devil, because God was with him.[1495]

Better is one day in your courts than a thousand elsewhere; I would rather be a doorkeeper in the house of my God than dwell in the tents of the wicked.[1496]

But do not forget this one thing, dear friends: With the Lord a day is like a thousand years, and a thousand years are like a day.[1497]

For the Lord God is a sun and shield; the Lord bestows favor and honor; no good thing does he withhold from those whose walk is blameless.[1498]

If you, then, though you are evil, know how to give good gifts to your children, how much more will your Father in heaven give good gifts to those who ask him![1499]

Lord Almighty, blessed is the one who trusts in you.[1500]

May the God of hope fill you with all joy and peace as you trust in him, so that you may overflow with hope by the power of the Holy Spirit.[1501]

Psalm 95

Come, let us sing for joy to the Lord; let us shout aloud to the Rock of our salvation.[1502]

Sing to the Lord, all the earth; proclaim his salvation day after day.[1503]

Let us come before him with thanksgiving and extol him with music and song.[1504]

Sing and make music from your heart to the Lord, always giving thanks to God the Father for everything, in the name of our Lord Jesus Christ.[1505]

For the Lord is the great God, the great King above all gods.[1506]

"You are a king, then!" said Pilate. Jesus answered, "You say that I am a king. In fact, the reason I was born and came into the world is to testify to the truth.[1507]

In his hand are the depths of the earth, and the mountain peaks belong to him.[1508]

The Lord does whatever pleases him, in the heavens and on the earth, in the seas and all their depths.[1509]

The sea is his, for he made it, and his hands formed the dry land.[1510]

Through him all things were made; without him nothing was made that has been made.[1511]

Come, let us bow down in worship, let us kneel before the Lord our Maker;[1512]

Therefore God exalted him to the highest place and gave him the name that is above every name, that at the name of Jesus every knee should bow, in heaven and on earth and under the earth,[1513]

for he is our God and we are the people of his pasture, the flock under his care.[1514]

I am the gate; whoever enters through me will be saved. They will come in and go out, and find pasture.[1515]

Today, if only you would hear his voice,[1516]

Then a cloud appeared and covered them, and a voice came from the cloud: "This is my Son, whom I love. Listen to him!"[1517]

"Do not harden your hearts as you did at Meribah, as you did that day at Massah in the wilderness,[1518]

They are darkened in their understanding and separated from the life of God because of the ignorance that is in them due to the hardening of their hearts.[1519]

where your ancestors tested me; they tried me, though they had seen what I did.[1520]

We should not test Christ, as some of them did—and were killed by snakes.[1521]

For forty years I was angry with that generation; I said, 'They are a people whose hearts go astray, and they have not known my ways.'[1522]

And with whom was he angry for forty years? Was it not with those who sinned, whose bodies perished in the wilderness?[1523]

So I declared on oath in my anger, 'They shall never enter my rest.'"[1524]

Therefore, since the promise of entering his rest still stands, let us be careful that none of you be found to have fallen short of it.[1525]

Psalm 138

I will praise you, Lord, with all my heart; before the "gods" I will sing your praise.[1526]

For even if there are so-called gods, whether in heaven or on earth (as indeed there are many "gods" and many "lords"), yet for us there is but one God, the Father, from whom all things came and for whom we live; and there is but one Lord, Jesus Christ, through whom all things came and through whom we live.[1527]

I will bow down toward your holy temple and will praise your name for your unfailing love and your faithfulness,[1528]

I tell you that something greater than the temple is here.[1529]

for you have so exalted your solemn decree that it surpasses your fame.[1530]

For no matter how many promises God has made, they are "Yes" in Christ. And so through him the "Amen" is spoken by us to the glory of God.[1531]

When I called, you answered me; you greatly emboldened me.[1532]

Then you will call, and the Lord will answer; you will cry for help, and he will say: Here am I.[1533]

May all the kings of the earth praise you, Lord, when they hear what you have decreed.[1534]

Grace and peace to you from him who is, and who was, and who is to come, and from the seven spirits before his throne, and from Jesus Christ, who is the faithful witness, the firstborn from the dead, and the ruler of the kings of the earth.[1535]

May they sing of the ways of the Lord, for the glory of the Lord is great.[1536]

And they were calling to one another: "Holy, holy, holy is the Lord Almighty; the whole earth is full of his glory."[1537]

Though the Lord is exalted, he looks kindly on the lowly; though lofty, he sees them from afar.[1538]

For this is what the high and exalted One says—he who lives forever, whose name is holy: "I live in a high and holy place, but also with the one who is contrite and lowly in spirit, to revive the spirit of the lowly and to revive the heart of the contrite.[1539]

Though I walk in the midst of trouble, you preserve my life.[1540]

The Lord is a refuge for the oppressed, a stronghold in times of trouble.[1541]

You stretch out your hand against the anger of my foes; with your right hand you save me.[1542]

So do not fear, for I am with you; do not be dismayed, for I am your God. I will strengthen you and help you; I will uphold you with my righteous right hand.[1543]

The Lord will vindicate me; your love, Lord, endures forever—do not abandon the works of your hands.[1544]

being confident of this, that he who began a good work in you will carry it on to completion until the day of Christ Jesus.[1545]

Psalm 139

You have searched me, Lord, and you know me. You know when I sit and when I rise; you perceive my thoughts from afar.[1546]

And even the very hairs of your head are all numbered.[1547]

You discern my going out and my lying down; you are familiar with all my ways. Before a word is on my tongue you, Lord, know it completely.[1548]

Nothing in all creation is hidden from God's sight. Everything is uncovered and laid bare before the eyes of him to whom we must give account.[1549]

You hem me in behind and before, and you lay your hand upon me. Such knowledge is too wonderful for me, too lofty for me to attain.[1550]

David said about him: "'I saw the Lord always before me. Because he is at my right hand, I will not be shaken.[1551]

Where can I go from your Spirit? Where can I flee from your presence? If I go up to the heavens, you are there; if I make my bed in the depths, you are there.[1552]

And surely I am with you always, to the very end of the age."[1553]

If I rise on the wings of the dawn, if I settle on the far side of the sea, even there your hand will guide me, your right hand will hold me fast.[1554]

I give them eternal life, and they shall never perish; no one will snatch them out of my hand.[1555]

If I say, "Surely the darkness will hide me and the light become night around me," even the darkness will not be dark to you; the night will shine like the day, for darkness is as light to you.[1556]

God is light; in him there is no darkness at all.[1557]

For you created my inmost being; you knit me together in my mother's womb. I praise you because I am fearfully and wonderfully made; your works are wonderful, I know that full well.[1558]

He chose to give us birth through the word of truth, that we might be a kind of firstfruits of all he created.[1559]

My frame was not hidden from you when I was made in the secret place, when I was woven together in the depths of the earth. Your eyes saw my unformed body; all the days ordained for me were written in your book before one of them came to be.[1560]

Praise be to the God and Father of our Lord Jesus Christ, who has blessed us in the heavenly realms with every spiritual blessing in Christ. For he chose us in him before the creation of the world to be holy and blameless in his sight.[1561]

How precious to me are your thoughts, God! How vast is the sum of them! Were I to count them, they would outnumber the grains of sand—when I awake, I am still with you.[1562]

Oh, the depth of the riches of the wisdom and knowledge of God! How unsearchable his judgments, and his paths beyond tracing out! "Who has known the mind of the Lord?[1563]

If only you, God, would slay the wicked! Away from me, you who are bloodthirsty! They speak of you with evil intent; your adversaries misuse your name.[1564]

The Lord is not slow in keeping his promise, as some understand slowness. Instead he is patient with you, not wanting anyone to perish, but everyone to come to repentance.[1565]

Do I not hate those who hate you, Lord, and abhor those who are in rebellion against you? I have nothing but hatred for them; I count them my enemies.[1566]

For, as I have often told you before and now tell you again even with tears, many live as enemies of the cross of Christ.[1567]

Search me, God, and know my heart; test me and know my anxious thoughts. See if there is any offensive way in me, and lead me in the way everlasting.[1568]

We are not trying to please people but God, who tests our hearts.[1569]

Psalm 150

Praise the Lord. Praise God in his sanctuary;[1570]

We have this hope as an anchor for the soul, firm and secure. It enters the inner sanctuary behind the curtain, where our forerunner, Jesus, has entered on our behalf.[1571]

praise him in his mighty heavens.[1572]

For Christ did not enter a sanctuary made with human hands that was only a copy of the true one; he entered heaven itself, now to appear for us in God's presence.[1573]

Praise him for his acts of power;[1574]

Immediately her bleeding stopped and she felt in her body that she was freed from her suffering. At once Jesus realized that power had gone out from him. He turned around in the crowd and asked, "Who touched my clothes?[1575]

praise him for his surpassing greatness.[1576]

I will proclaim the name of the Lord. Oh, praise the greatness of our God![1577]

Praise him with the sounding of the trumpet,[1578]

God has ascended amid shouts of joy, the Lord amid the sounding of trumpets. [1579]

praise him with the harp and lyre,[1580]

And I heard a sound from heaven like the roar of rushing waters and like a loud peal of thunder. The sound I heard was like that of harpists playing their harps.[1581]

praise him with timbrel and dancing,[1582]

Then Miriam the prophet, Aaron's sister, took a timbrel in her hand, and all the women followed her, with timbrels and dancing. Miriam sang to them: "Sing to the Lord, for he is highly exalted.[1583]

praise him with the strings and pipe,[1584]

Sing to him a new song; play skillfully, and shout for joy.[1585]

praise him with the clash of cymbals,[1586]

The trumpeters and musicians joined in unison to give praise and thanks to the Lord. Accompanied by trumpets, cymbals and other instruments, the singers raised their voices in praise to the Lord and sang: "He is good; his love endures forever."[1587]

praise him with resounding cymbals.[1588]

 At the dedication of the wall of Jerusalem, the Levites were sought out from where they lived and were brought to Jerusalem to celebrate joyfully the dedication with songs of thanksgiving and with the music of cymbals, harps and lyres.[1589]

Let everything that has breath praise the Lord. Praise the Lord.[1590]

My mouth will speak in praise of the Lord. Let every creature praise his holy name for ever and ever.[1591]

Footnotes

[1] James 2:21 (NIV)

[2] Genesis 22:11 (NIV)

[3] Luke 17:29 (NIV)

[4] Genesis 19:1 (NIV)

[5] Luke 20:37 (NIV)

[6] Exodus 3:2 (NIV)

[7] Daniel 6:16 (NIV)

[8] Daniel 6:22ab (NIV)

[9] Psalm 7:10 (NIV)

[10] Daniel 3:28a (NIV)

[11] 2 Peter 2:15 (NIV)

[12] Numbers 22:31 (NIV)

[13] Isaiah 7:14 (NIV)

[14] Luke 1:26-27(NIV)

[15] John 7:42 (NIV)

[16] Luke 2:15 (NIV)

[17] John 19:41 (NIV)

[18] Matthew 28:2 (NIV)

[19] Jeremiah 40:4a (NIV)

[20] Acts 12:7 (NIV) |

[21] Acts 8:36 (NIV)

22 Acts 8:26 (NIV)

23 1 Chronicles 16:25 (NIV)

24 Revelation 5:2 (NIV)

25 Exodus 34:14 (NIV)

26 Deuteronomy 6:15 (NIV)

27 Hebrews 12:28-29 (NIV)

28 Exodus 15:7 (NIV)

29 1 Thessalonians 5:9 (NIV)

30 Romans 2:8 (NIV)

31 Matthew 21:12 (NIV)

32 Psalm 90:11 (NIV)

33 Matthew 26:59 (NIV)

34 Matthew 3:7 (NIRV)

35 2 Peter 3:9 (NIV)

36 Exodus 34:6 (NIV)

37 Ephesians 4:29 (NIV)

38 James 1:19-20 (NIV)

39 Psalm 4:4 (NIV)

40 Ephesians 4:26-27 (NIV)

41Hebrews 12:11 (NIV)

42 Jeremiah 10:24 (NIV)

43 1 Thessalonians 1:9b-10 (NIV)

44 Isaiah 13:9 (NIV)

45 Revelation 19:15 (NIV)

46 Psalm 56:7 (NIV)

47 Revelation 21:4 (NIV)

48 Psalm 30:5 (NIV)

49 Luke 6:14-16 (NIV)

50 Revelation 21:14 (NIV)

51 Deuteronomy 13:4 (NIV)

52 Acts 5:29 (NIV)

53 Psalm 7:7 (NIV)

54 Mark 6:30 (NIV)

55 Matthew 28:5-6 (NIV)

56 Acts 4:2 (NIV)

57 Luke 24:49 (NIV)

58 Acts 2:43 (NIV)

59 Psalm 106:3 (NIV)

60 Acts 2:42 (NIV)

61 2 Corinthians 9:11 (NIV)

62 Acts 4:34b-35 (NIV)

63 Acts 12:1-2 (NIV)

64 Luke 11:49 (NIV)

65 1 Peter 4:16 (NIV)

66 Acts 5:41 (NIV)

67 John 3:30 (NIV)

[68] Luke 17:5 (NIV)

[69] 1 Corinthians 4:1 (NIV)

[70] 2 Timothy 1:11 (NIV)

[71] Zechariah 14:4 (NIV)

[72] Acts 1:12 (NIV)

[73] John 8:58 (NIV)

[74] John 14:1 (NIV)

[75] Isaiah 53:11 (NIV)

[76] John 11:27 (NIV)

[77] Hebrews 12:1b-2 (NIV)

[78] Romans 3:22a (NIV)

[79] 1 Peter 1:20 (NIV)

[80] Isaiah 53:1 (NIV)

[81] Hebrews 13:9a (NIV)

[82] Proverbs 14:15 (NIV)

[83] Psalm 34:11 (NIV)

[84] John 1:12 (NIV)

[85] 2 Corinthians 4:4 (NIV)

[86] John 6:36 (NIV)

[87] Isaiah 35:5 (NIV)

[88] Matthew 9:28 (NIV)

[89] Acts 22:15 (NIV)

[90] Isaiah 43:10a (NIV)

91 Job 9:10 (NIV)

92 John 4:48 (NIV)

93 Job 34:4 (NIV)

94 John 4:42 (NIV)

95 1 Corinthians 15:58 (NIV)

96 John 6:29 (NIV)

97 Psalm 55:4 (NIV)

98 Luke 22:44 (NIV)

99 Isaiah 53:5 (NIV)

100 Colossians 1:19-20 (NIV)

101 Romans 4:8 (NIV)

102 Revelation 1:5b-6 (NIV)

103 Psalm 111:9 (NIV)

104 Ephesians 1:7-8a (NIV)

105 Psalm 145:18 (NIV)

106 Ephesians 2:13 (NIV)

107 Jeremiah 31:31 (NIV)

108 1 Corinthians 11:25 (NIV)

109 Psalm 51:2 (NIV)

110 Hebrews 9:14 (NIV)

111 Psalm 23:1 (NIV)

112 Hebrews 13:20-21 (NIV)

113 Job 25:4 (NIV)

114 Romans 5:9 (NIV)

115 Isaiah 1:18 (NIV)

116 Revelation 7:14bc (NIV)

117 1 John 5:11 (NIV)

118 John 6:54 (NIV)

119 Isaiah 40:28abc (NIV)

120 Psalm 90:2 (NIV)

121 Genesis 2:22 (NIV)

122 1 Corinthians 11:12 (NIV)

123 Psalm 139:16 (NIV)

124 Jeremiah 1:5a (NIV)

125 Psalm 31:15a (NIV)

126 Ecclesiastes 3:2 (NIV)

127 Ecclesiastes 7:20 (NIV)

128 Job 15:14 (NIV)

129 Isaiah 11:1 (NIV)

130 Luke 2:11 (NIV)

131 Colossians 1:17 (NIV)

132 John 8:58 (NIV)

133 Isaiah 35:5 (NIV)

134 John 9:32 (NIV)

135 John 20:31 (NIV)

136 1 John 5:1 (NIV)

137 Titus 3:5b (NIV)

138 John 3:3 (NIV)

139 Hebrews 4:12 (NIV)

140 1 Peter 1:23 (NIV)

141 Psalm 36:7 (NIV)

142 1 John 4:7 (NIV)

143 James 1:17 (NIV)

144 Psalm 127:3 (NIV)

145 Numbers 6:24 (NIV)

146 Proverbs 17:6 (NIV)

147 Proverbs 9:10 (NIV)

148 Psalm 34:11 (NIV)

149 2 Timothy 3:16-17 (NIV)

150 Deuteronomy 6:7 (NIV)

151 John 3:16 (NIV)

152 1 John 3:1a (NIV)

153 Daniel 7:27a (NIV)

154 Matthew 19:14 (NIV)

155 Isaiah 50:10 (NIV)

156 John 12:36a (NIV)

157 Psalm 34:14 (NIV)

158 Matthew 5:9 (NIV)

159 Job 5:17 (NIV)

[160] Hebrews 12:7 (NIV)

[161] Psalm 52:7 (NIV)

[162] Mark 10:24-25 (NIV)

[163] Job 16:19 (NIV)

[164] 1 John 2:1 (NIV

[165] Isaiah 5:7a (NIV)

[166] Psalm 135:4 (NIV)

[167] Acts 3:13a (NIV)

[168] Isaiah 42:1 (NIV)

[169] Acts 4:11 (NIV)

[170] 1 Peter 2:6 (NIV)

[171] 1 John 4:14 (NIV)

[172] Luke 23:35 (NIV)

[173] Isaiah 9:2 (NIV)

[174] 1 Peter 2:9 (NIV)

[175] Romans 8:29 (NIV)

[176] Matthew 22:14 (NIV)

[177] Romans 8:1 (NIV)

[178] Romans 8:33 (NIV)

[179] Ephesians 4:1-2 (NIV)

[180] Colossians 3:12 (NIV)

[181] 1 Peter 3:17 (NIV)

[182] Luke 18:7 (NIV)

183 John 17:17 (NIV)

184 Psalm 119:30 (NIV)

185 Job 12:13 (NIV)

186 Luke 9:35 (NIV)

187 Revelation 19:14 (NIV)

188 Revelation 17:14 (NIV)

189 Psalm 102:25 (NIV)

190 Genesis 1:1 (NIV)

191 Deuteronomy 4:39 (NIV)

192 Colossians 1:16 (NIV)

193 1 Chronicles 29:11 (NIV)

194 Revelation 4:11 (NIV)

195 Psalm 33:6 (NIV)

196 Isaiah 40:26 (NIV)

197 Job 28:25 (NIV)

198 Amos 4:13 (NIV)

199 Mark 10:6 (NIV)

200 Genesis 1:27 (NIV)

201 Acts 17:26 (NIV)

202 Isaiah 45:18 (NIV)

203 Genesis 3:22a (NIV)

204 Ezekiel 28:15 (NIV)

205 Romans 10:9–10 (NIV)

206 Psalm 51:10 (NIV)

207 2 Corinthians 5:17 (NIV)

208 Ephesians 4:24 (NIV)

209 John 9:4 (NIV)

210 Ephesians 2:10 (NIV)

211 1 Corinthians 2:9 (NIV)

212 Isaiah 65:17 (NIV)

213 1 Samuel 2:10bc (NIV)

214 1 Samuel 16:13a (NIV)

215 1 Samuel 17:4 (NIV)

216 1 Samuel 17:50 (NIV)

217 Psalm 59:3 (NIV)

218 1 Samuel 19:11a (NIV)

219 1 Samuel 24:10a (NIV)

220 1 Samuel 24:4b (NIV)

221 Psalm 2:6 (NIV)

222 2 Samuel 5:7 (NIV)

223 2 Samuel 11:3b (NIV)

224 2 Samuel 12:13a (NIV)

225 Psalm 3:1 (NIV)

226 2 Samuel 15:13 (NIV)

227 2 Samuel 18:33 (NIV)

228 2 Samuel 18:32 (NIRV)

229 Psalm 41:4 (NIV)

230 2 Samuel 24:10 (NIV)

231 1 Kings 1:39 (NIV)

232 1 Chronicles 29:23a (NIV)

233 1 Chronicles 29:28a (NIV)

234 Acts 13:36 (NIV)

235 Jeremiah 30:21a (NIV)

236 Hosea 3:5 (NIV)

237 Genesis 1:1 (NIV)

238 Romans 1:20 (NIV)

239 Revelation 19:16 (NIV)

240 1 Timothy 1:17 (NIV)

241 Psalm 62:2 (NIV)

242 Isaiah 26:4 (NIV)

243 1 Chronicles 16:25 (NIV)

244 Psalm 111:10 (NIV)

245 Romans 8:6 (NIV)

246 Galatians 6:8 (NIV)

247 Isaiah 1:11 (NIV)

248 Hebrews 9:12 (NIV)

249 1 Corinthians 15:3-4 (NIV)

250 Revelation 14:6 (NIV)

251 Psalm 8:4 (NIV)

[252] Psalm 16:11 (NIV)

[253] Romans 8:18 (NIV)

[254] 2 Corinthians 4:17 (NIV)

[255] John 1:14 (NIV)

[256] Psalm 119:89 (NIV)

[257] 1 Peter 1:8 (NIV)

[258] Hebrews 11:1 (NIV)

[259] Galatians 3:2 (NIV)

[260] Romans 10:17 (NIV)

[261] Deuteronomy 32:4a (NIV)

[262] Hebrews 12:1-2a (NIV)

[263] 1 Thessalonians 5:9 (NIV)

[264] Ephesians 2:8 (NIV)

[265] Genesis 22:1-2(NIV)

[266] 1 Peter 1:7 (NIV)

[267] Exodus 3:11 (NIV)

[268] Matthew 8:26a (NIV)

[269] 1 Samuel 17:45 (NIRV)

[270] 1 Corinthians 16:13 (NIV)

[271] Daniel 6:23 (NIV)

[272] Psalm 86:2 (NIV)

[273] Psalm 147:5 (NIV)

[274] 1 Corinthians 2:4-5 (NIV)

275 Acts 7:59 (NIV)

276 2 Timothy 4:7 (NIV)

277 1 Peter 5:8 (NIV)

278 Ephesians 6:16 (NIV)

279 Revelation 6:10 (NIV)

280 Luke 18:8 (NIV)

281 Isaiah 43:25 (NIV)

282 Hebrews 8:12 (NIV)

283 Psalm 62:1 (NIV)

284 Mark 2:7c (NIV)

285 Jeremiah 31:31 (NIV)

286 Matthew 26:28 (NIV)

287 Ephesians 2:13 (NIV)

288 Hebrews 9:22 (NIV)

289 Isaiah 53:5 (NIV)

290 Romans 4:7 (NIV)

291 Psalm 22:18 (NIV)

292 Luke 23:34 (NIV)

293 Matthew 1:21 (NIV)

294 Psalm 79:9 (NIV)

295 Romans 10:9 (NIV)

296 1 John 2:12 (NIV)

297 2 Peter 3:9 (NIV)

298 Acts 2:38a (NIV)

299 Psalm 32:5 (NIV)

300 1 John 1:9 (NIV)

301 Proverbs 19:11 (NIV)

302 Colossians 3:13 (NIV)

303 Hebrews 4:13 (NIV)

304 Psalm 19:12 (NIV)

305 Romans 6:23 (NIV)

306 Genesis 2:16-17 (NIV)

307 Romans 7:24 (NIV)

308 John 8:36 (NIV)

309 1 Peter 3:18 (NIV)

310 Colossians 1:22 (NIV)

311 1 John 5:5 (NIV)

312 Acts 13:39a (NIV)

313 Deuteronomy 10:17 (NIV)

314 Galatians 3:28 (NIV)

315 John 14:6 (NIV)

316 John 8:32 (NIV)

317 James 1:27a (NIV)

318 Psalm 112:9 (NIV)

319 1 Timothy 6:18 (NIV)

320 Psalm 112:5 (NIV)

321 1 Peter 4:10 (NIV)

322 Galatians 5:13 (NIV)

323 1 Timothy 6:10 (NIV)

324 Hebrews 13:5 (NIV)

325 1 Peter 3:10 (NIV)

326 Proverbs 4:24 (NIV)

327 John 4:10 (NIV)

328 Revelation 22:17 (NIV)

329 Revelation 22:13 (NIV)

330 Psalm 90:2 (NIV)

331 Habakkuk 1:13a (NIV)

332 Psalm 99:9 (NIV)

333 Malachi 3:6 (NIV)

334 Hebrews 6:17 (NIV)

335 Job 42:2 (NIV)

336 Revelation 19:6 (NIV)

337 Jeremiah 23:24 (NIV)

338 1 Kings 8:27 (NIV)

339 Psalm 147:5 (NIV)

340 1 John 3:20 (NIV)

341 Psalm 119:68 (NIV)

342 Mark 10:18 (NIV)

343 Psalm 13:5 (NIV)

344 1 John 4:8 (NIV)

345 Psalm 71:20 (NIV)

346 1 Peter 5:10 (NIV)

347 Psalm 41:4 (NIV)

348 Ephesians 2:4-5 (NIV)

349 Jeremiah 29:12 (NIV)

350 Revelation 8:4 (NIV)

351 John 1:14a (NIV)

352 Revelation 21:3 (NIV)

353 Revelation 1:8 (NIV)

354 Job 36:26 (NIV)

355 Leviticus 11:44a (NIV)

356 Psalm 77:13 (NIV)

357 Psalm 74:12 (NIV)

358 Psalm 95:3 (NIV)

359 Micah 4:5 (NIV)

360 Malachi 1:11a (NIV)

361 2 Samuel 22:4 (NIV)

362 1 Chronicles 16:25 (NIV)

363 Psalm 136:26 (NIV)

364 Daniel 9:4b (NIV)

365 Psalm 140:6 (NIV)

366 2 Samuel 24:14 (NIV)

367 Luke 4:8 (NIV)

368 Nehemiah 8:6 (NIV)

369 Psalm 25:8 NIV)

370 Luke 5:29 NIV)

371 John 21:15 (NIV)

372 John 6:5 (NIV)

373 Isaiah 53:7 (NIV)

374 Matthew 27:14 (NIV)

375 Psalm 14:2 (NIV)

376 Hebrews 4:14 (NIV)

377 Psalm 148:3,5 (NIV)

378 Psalm 33:6 (NIV)

379 Psalm 145:10 (NIV)

380 Psalm 19:1 (NIV)

381 Psalm 68:5 (NIV)

382 Psalm 121:2 (NIV)

383 Revelation 5:13b (NIV)

384 Psalm 103:19 NIV)

385 1 John 4:14 (NIV)

386 Matthew 3:17 (NIV)

387 Revelation 12:10b (NIV)

388 Matthew 4:17 (NIV)

389 John 6:68 (NIV)

390 Psalm 73:25 (NIV)

391 Colossians 3:1 (NIV)

392 Matthew 6:19-20 (NIV)

393 Isaiah 55:11 (NIV)

394 Matthew 24:35 (NIV)

395 Matthew 24:27 (NIV)

396 Daniel 7:13a (NIV)

397 Revelation 19:15 (NIV)

398 Romans 1:18 (NIV)

399 1 Corinthians 2:9 (NIV)

400 Isaiah 65:17 (NIV)

401 Habakkuk 1:13a (NIV)

402 Revelation 4:8 (NIV)

403 Psalm 148:2 (NIV)

404 Psalm 89:7 (NIV)

405 John 1:46a (NIV)

406 Mark 1:24 (NIV)

407 2 Corinthians 1:21b-22 (NIV)

408 Ephesians 1:13b-14 (NIV)

409 2 John 1:6 (NIV)

410 Deuteronomy 28:9 (NIV)

411 John 8:12 (NIV)

412 1 Peter 2:9 (NIV)

413 Luke 22:69 (NIV)

414 Psalm 47:8 (NIV)

415 Acts 3:6 (NIV)

416 Acts 4:30 (NIV)

417 Romans 12:2a (NIV)

418 1 Thessalonians 4:7 (NIV)

419 Psalm 50:14 (NIV)

420 Romans 12:1 (NIV)

421 Psalm 66:2 (NIV)

422 Psalm 105:3 (NIV)

423 1 Corinthians (16:13)

424 Psalm 31:24 (NIV)

425 Matthew 11:29 (NIV)

426 Psalm 62:5 (NIV)

427 Psalm 145:6 (NIV)

428 Psalm 65:5(NIV)

429 Proverbs 30:5 (NIV)

430 Psalm 33:20 (NIV)

431 Psalm 33:4 (NIV)

432 Psalm 119:114 (NIV)

433 Psalm 119:41 (NIV)

434 Psalm 119:116 (NIV)

435 Psalm 150:6a (NIV)

436 Psalm 42: 5 (NIV)

437 Psalm 16:9 (NIV)

438 Job 11:18 (NIV)

439 Philippians 2:9-10 (NIV)

440 Matthew 12:21 (NIV)

441 John 3:3 (NIV)

442 1 Peter 1:3 (NIV)

443 Proverbs 15:16 (NIV)

444 1 Timothy 6:17 (NIV)

445 Colossians 4:6 (NIV)

446 1 Peter 3:15b (NIV)

447 Hosea 12:3 (NIV)

448 Genesis 25:26a (NIV)

449 Hebrews 12:16 (NIV)

450 Genesis 25:33 (NIV)

451 Proverbs 26:24 (NIV)

452 Genesis 27:19 (NIV)

453 1 Corinthians 13:4a (NIV)

454 Genesis 29:18 (NIV)

455 Genesis 49:28 (NIV)

456 Genesis 35:22b (NIV)

457 Hosea 12:4a (NIV)

458 Genesis 32:28 (NIV)

459 Genesis 32:11 (NIV)

460 Genesis 33:4 (NIV)

461 Romans 12:19 (NIV)

462 Genesis 34:25 (NIV)

463 Genesis 35:18 (NIV)

464 Genesis 35:20 (NIV)

465 Genesis 37:3 (NIV)

466 Psalm 77:15 (NIV)

467 Genesis 49:29 (NIV)

468 Matthew 22:32 (NIV)

469 Isaiah 7:14 (NIV)

470 Matthew 1:18 (NIV)

471 Isaiah 11:2 (NIV)

472 Matthew 3:16 (NIV)

473 Hebrews 4:15 (NIV)

474 Luke 4:1-2a (NIV)

475 Exodus 24:17 (NIV)

476 Matthew 17:1-2 (NIV)

477 John 5:25 (NIV)

478 John 11:43-44 (NIV)

479 Isaiah 24:16 (NIV)

480 Matthew 26:20-21 (NIV)

481 Isaiah 53:5 (NIV)

482 Luke 23:46 (NIV)

483 2 Corinthians 13:4a (NIV)

484 Mark 16:6 (NIV)

485 Daniel 7:14a (NIV)

486 Matthew 28:18-19 (NIV)

487 Acts 1:9 (NIV)

488 John 7:33 (NIV)

489 Luke 21:27 (NIV)

490 Titus 2:13 (NIRV)

491 Revelation 21:1 (NIV)

492 John 17:3 (NIV)

493 Jeremiah 1:5ab (NIV)

494 Genesis 30:22-24 (NIV)

495 Proverbs 27:4 (NIV)

496 Genesis 37:23-24a (NIV)

497 Matthew 5:27-28 (NIV)

498 Genesis 39:7 (NIV)

499 Psalm 84:11 (NIV)

500 Genesis 39:20b-21 (NIV)

501 John 3:21 (NIV)

502 Genesis 41:15 (NIV)

503 1 Samuel 26:23a (NIV)

504 Genesis 41:41 (NIV)

505 Job 36:31 (NIV)

506 Genesis 41:48a (NIV)

507 Psalm 37:19 (NIV)

508 Genesis 41:53-54a (NIV)

509 Proverbs 11:26 (NIV)

510 Genesis 42:6 (NIV)

511 Luke 15:24 (NIV)

512 Genesis 46:30 (NIV)

513 Job 42:2 (NIV)

514 Genesis 50:19-20 (NIV)

515 Acts 7:35 ((NIV)

516 Genesis 50:24 (NIV)

517 Psalm 19:1 (NIV)

518 Psalm 92:4 (NIV)

519 Genesis 2:1 (NIV)

520 Psalm 66:1 (NIV)

521 Psalm 89:15 (NIV)

522 Psalm 21:6 (NIV)

523 Romans 5:12 (NIV)

524 James 4:9 (NIV)

525 Hebrews 1:3 (NIV)

526 Psalm 118:15 (NIV)

527 1 Corinthians 10:3-4 (NIV)

[528] Psalm 95:1 (NIV)

[529] Matthew 6:21 (NIV)

[530] Matthew 13:44 (NIV)

[531] Hebrews 12:28 (NIV)

[532] Psalm 100:2 (NIV)

[533] Proverbs 4:11 (NIV)

[534] Acts 2:28 (NIV)

[535] Matthew 5:10 (NIV)

[536] James 1:2-3 (NIV)

[537] Hebrews 10:14 (NIV)

[538] Jude 1:24 (NIV)

[539] 2 Samuel 7:22 (NIV)

[540] Matthew 6:9b-10 (NIV)

[541] Psalm 83:18 (NIV)

[542] Isaiah 37:16a (NIV)

[543] Psalm 60:5 (NIV)

[544] 2 Kings 19:19 (NIV)

[545] Isaiah 12:5 (NIV)

[546] Psalm 68:32 (NIV)

[547] Psalm 149:4 (NIV)

[548] Matthew 5:3 (NIV)

[549] 2 Corinthians 4:8-9 (NIV)

[550] Matthew 5:10 (NIV)

551 Psalm 145:18 (NIV)

552 Matthew 10:7 (NIV)

553 Matthew 17:20b (NIV)

554 Matthew 13:31b (NIV)

555 Matthew 16:12 (NIV)

556 Matthew 13:33b (NIV)

557 Isaiah 45:3 (NIV)

558 Matthew 13:44a (NIV)

559 Matthew 25:32 (NIV)

560 Matthew 13:47-48 (NIV)

561 1 John 2:17 (NIV)

562 Matthew 7:21 (NIV)

563 Psalm 23:1 (NIV)

564 Luke 12:27 (NIV)

565 Romans 8:20-21 (NIV)

566 Genesis 5:29 (NIV)

567 Hebrews 4:9-10 (NIV)

568 Deuteronomy 5:13-14a (NIV)

569 Ephesians 5:15-16 (NIV)

570 Ecclesiastes 5:18 (NIV)

571 Genesis 3:19 (NIV)

572 Psalm 104:23 (NIV)

573 Isaiah 3:10 (NIV)

[574] Psalm 128:2 (NIV)

[575] Proverbs 27:17 (NIV)

[576] Ecclesiastes 4:9-10a (NIV)

[577] 1 Corinthians 3:11 (NIV)

[578] Psalm 127:1 (NIV)

[579] 2 Chronicles 15:7 (NIV)

[580] 1 Corinthians 15:58 (NIV)

[581] Matthew 16:27 (NIV)

[582] Ecclesiastes 1:3 NIV)

[583] Psalm 73:7-8 (NIV)

[584] Psalm 2:4 (NIV)

[585] Proverbs 21:24 (NIV)

[586] Psalm 37:13 (NIV)

[587] Jeremiah 49:14 (NIV)

[588] Psalm 59:8 (NIV)

[589] Romans 15:13 (NIV)

[590] Job 8:21 (NIV)

[591] Luke 18:27 (NIV)

[592] Genesis 17:17 (NIV)

[593] Galatians 4:28 (NIV)

[594] Genesis 21:6 (NIV)

[595] Romans 1:21 (NIV)

[596] James 4:9 (NIV)

597 Romans 14:22b (NIV)

598 Proverbs 14:13 (NIV)

599 Romans 12:15 (NIV)

600 Ecclesiastes 3:4 (NIV)

601 Psalm 20:1 (NIV)

602 Job 5:22 (NIV)

603 Psalm 58:11 (NIV)

604 Luke 6:21 (NIV))

605 Psalm 33:9 (NIV)

606 Genesis 1:3 (NIV)

607 1 Corinthians 15:41 (NIV)

608 Genesis 1:16 (NIV)

609 Job 33:4 (NIV)

610 Psalm 13:3 (NIV)

611 Psalm 139:13 (NIV)

612 Proverbs 20:27 (NIV)

613 Proverbs 4:19 (NIV)

614 2 Corinthians 4:4 (NIV)

615 Luke 2:11 (NIV)

616 Matthew 4:16 (NIV)

617 John 14:6 (NIV)

618 Job 38:19a (NIV)

619 Psalm 68:19 (NIV)

620 Matthew 11:30 (NIV)

621 Job 11:16 (NIV)

622 2 Corinthians 4:17 (NIV)

623 1 Peter 4:10 (NIV)

624 James 1:17 (NIV)

625 Acts 2:28 (NIV)

626 Psalm 89:15 (NIV)

627 Malachi 3:2 (NIV)

628 1 Corinthians 3:13 (NIV)

629 Ecclesiastes 11:5 (NIV)

630 Amos 4:13 (NIV)

631 Psalm 48:10 (NIV)

632 Psalm 7:17 (NIV)

633 Psalm 90:2 (NIV)

634 Isaiah 40:28abc (NIV)

635 1 Timothy 6:17 (NIV)

636 Genesis 22:14 (NIV)

637 Song of Songs 2:4 (NIV)

638 Exodus 17:15 (NIV)

639 Luke 2:14 (NIV)

640 Judges 6:24a (NIV)

641 Psalm 144:9-10 (NIV)

642 1 Samuel 17:45 (NIV)

643 Revelation 7:17ab (NIV)

644 Psalm 23:1 (NIV)

645 1 Corinthians 1:30 NIV)

646 Jeremiah 23:6 (NIV)

647 Revelation 21:2 (NIV)

648 Ezekiel 48:35 (NIV)

649 1 John 4:14 (NIV)

650 John 3:16 (NIV)

651 Colossians 1:19 (NIV)

652 Matthew 3:17 (NIV)

653 Proverbs 4:19 (NIV)

654 John 3:19 (NIV)

655 John 8:12 (NIV)

656 Colossians 1:13 (NIV)

657 Romans 3:23 (NIV)

658 Romans 5:8 (NIV)

659 Romans 3:25a (NIV)

660 1 John 4:10 (NIV)

661 John 19:30 (NIV)

662 1 John 3:16a (NIV)

663 Mark 10:17 (NIV)

664 1 John 5:1 (NIV)

665 Ephesians 2:8-9 (NIV)

[666] Galatians 2:20b (NIV)

[667] 2 Timothy 3:16-17 (NIV)

[668] 1 John 2:5a (NIV)

[669] Hebrews 12:7 (NIV)

[670] Proverbs 3:11-12 (NIV)

[671] 1 Thessalonians 4:17 (NIV)

[672] Psalm 23:6 (NIV)

[673] Isaiah 63:1b (NIV)

[674] Psalm 96:6 (NIV)

[675] Psalm 89:6 (NIV)

[676] Psalm 68:34 (NIV)

[677] Deuteronomy 32:4 (NIV)

[678] Psalm 145:5 (NIV)

[679] Psalm 50:3 (NIV)

[680] Deuteronomy 5:24a (NIV)

[681] Acts 4:24 (NIV)

[682] Isaiah 24:14 (NIV)

[683] Amos 5:8 (NIV)

[684] 1 Chronicles 29:11a (NIV)

[685] Titus 2:11 (NIV)

[686] Isaiah 26:10 (NIV)

[687] John 1:14b (NIV)

[688] 2 Peter 1:16 (NIV)

689 John 19:30 (NIV)

690 Hebrews 1:3 (NIV)

691 Revelation 6:16 (NIV)

692 Isaiah 2:19 (NIV)

693 Revelation 19:11 (NIV)

694 Psalm 45:4 (NIV)

695 Psalm 37:29 (NIV)

696 Jude 1:25 (NIV)

697 James 1:27 (NIV)

698 Hosea 6:6 (NIV)

699 Psalm 103:17 (NIV)

700 Luke 1:50 (NIV)

701 Isaiah 64:6 (NIV)

702 Titus 3:5 (NIV)

703 Jeremiah 17:14 (NIV)

704 Psalm 41:4 (NIV)

705 Isaiah 43:25 (NIV)

706 Psalm 51:1 (NIV)

707 Romans 10:9 (NIV)

708 Proverbs 28:13 (NIV) |

709 John 3:3 (NIV)

710 1 Peter 1:3-4a (NIV)

711 2 Peter 3:9 (NIV)

712 1 Timothy 1:16 (NIV)

713 1 John 5:14 (NIV)

714 Hebrews 4:16 (NIV)

715 1 Corinthians 6:15a (NIV)

716 Romans 12:1 (NIV)

717 Psalm 31:19 (NIV)

718 Jude 1:2 NIVV)

719 2 Samuel 22:17 (NIV)

720 Exodus 2:10 (NIV)

721 Psalm 104:4 (NIV)

722 Exodus 3:2 (NIV)

723 Psalm 78:50 (NIV)

724 Exodus 11:1 (NIV)

725 Hebrews 11:29 (NIV)

726 Exodus 14:13 (NIV)

727 John 6:58 (NIV)

728 Exodus 16:4a (NIV)

729 Deuteronomy 4:13 (NIV)

730 Exodus 31:18 (NIV)

731 Deuteronomy 9:7 (NIV)

732 Exodus 32:1a (NIV)

733 Isaiah 60:1 (NIV)

734 Exodus 34:29 (NIV)

735 Psalm 106:25 (NIV)

736 Numbers 21:8 (NIV)

737 Deuteronomy 32:52 (NIV)

738 Numbers 27:12 (NIV)

739 Deuteronomy 31:2a (NIV)

740 Deuteronomy 34:5 (NIV)

741 Mark 9:2 (NIV)

742 Luke 9:30 (NIV)

743 Genesis 1:1 (NIV)

744 Jeremiah 32:17 (NIV)

745 Revelation 4:11 (NIV)

746 John 1:3 (NIV)

747 Psalm 64:9 (NIV)

748 Ecclesiastes 3:14 (NIV)

749 Genesis 6:5 (NIV)

750 Psalm 101:4 (NIV)

751 Matthew 1:18 (NIV)

752 Philippians 2:6-7 (NIV)

753 Matthew 13:55-57 (NIV)

754 Isaiah 53:2 (NIV)

755 1 Peter 1:18-19 (NIV)

756 Isaiah 52:3 (NIV)

757 John 19:30 (NIV)

758 Daniel 9:26a (NIV)

759 2 Corinthians 4:4 (NIV)

760 Isaiah 44:18 (NIV)

761 John 14:6 (NIV)

762 John 15:5 (NIV)

763 2 Corinthians 5:10 (NIV)

764 Hebrews 4:13 (NIV)

765 Revelation 22:13 (NIV)

766 Revelation 1:4b (NIV)

767 Psalm 24:10 (NIV)

768 Luke 19:38 (NIV)

769 Proverbs 12:21 (NIV)

770 Isaiah 48:22 (NIV)

771 Isaiah 55:7 (NIV)

772 Psalm 34:14 (NIV)

773 Psalm 38:18 (NIV)

774 John 14:27 (NIV)

775 Romans 10:10 (NIV)

776 Romans 5:1 (NIV)

777 1 John 5:14 (NIV)

778 1 Samuel 1:17 (NIV)

779 Galatians 5:14 (NIV)

780 Romans 12:18 (NIV)

781 Psalm 68:32 (NIRV)

782 Isaiah 55:12 (NIV)

783 Galatians 6:9 (NIV)

784 James 3:18 (NIV)

785 Daniel 4:3b (NIV)

786 Isaiah 9:7a (NIV)

787 Hebrews 1:3 (NIV)

788 Colossians 1:19-21 (NIV)

789 Psalm 46:10 (NIV)

790 Job 36:22 (NIV))

791 Hebrews 4:13 (NIV)

792 Romans 1:20 (NIV)

793 Romans 3:23 (NIV)

794 1 Corinthians 15:56 (NIV)

795 1 Peter 5:8 (NIV)

796 Hebrews 2:14 (NIV)

797 1 Peter 1:3b (NIV)

798 Philippians 3:10 (NIV)

799 John 14:16 (NIV)

800 2 Timothy 1:7 (NIV)

801 2 Timothy 3:16 (NIV)

[802] Acts 19:20 (NIV)

[803] Luke 9:26 (NIV)

[804] Romans 1:16 (NIV)

[805] John 9:31 (NIV)

[806] James 5:16b (NIV)

[807] 1 Corinthians 1:27b (NIV)

[808] 2 Corinthians 12:9 (NIV)

[809] Job 10:9 (NIV)

[810] 2 Corinthians 4:7 (NIV)

[811] Revelation 1:7 (NIV)

[812] Luke 21:27 (NIV)

[813] Exodus 3:14a (NIV)

[814] Psalm 41:13 (NIV)

[815] Genesis 2:4 (NIV)

[816] 2 Chronicles 2:12b (NIV)

[817] Genesis 2:7 (NIV)

[818] Psalm 139:14a (NIV)

[819] Ephesians 2:1 (NIV)

[820] Psalm 6:5 (NIV)

[821] Luke 22:70 (NIV)

[822] Ephesians 1:3 (NIV)

[823] Romans 1:4 (NIV)

[824] Psalm 18:46 (NIV)

825 1 Peter 1:23 (NIV)

826 1 Peter 1:3 (NIV)

827 Psalm 32:11 (NIV)

828 Psalm 68:4 (NIV)

829 Psalm 33:18 (NIV)

830 Revelation 19:5 (NIV)

831 Deuteronomy 6:5 (NIV)

832 Psalm 86:12 (NIV)

833 Psalm 19:14 (NIV)

834 Psalm 119:108 (NIV)

835 Proverbs 25:21 (NIV)

836 Matthew 5:44 (NIV)

837 Romans 12:3b (NIV)

838 Matthew 6:5 (NIV)

839 Psalm 34:15 (NIV)

840 Matthew 6:6 (NIV)

841 Ecclesiastes 5:2 (NIV)

842 Matthew 6:7 (NIV)

843 Isaiah 57:15 (NIV)

844 Matthew 6:9 (NIV)

845 Genesis 3:6a (NIV)

846 Mark 14:38 (NIV)

847 Job 37:19 (NIV)

848 Romans 8:26 (NIV)

849 Job 27:10 (NIV)

850 Ephesians 6:18 (NIV)

851 Psalm 28:2 (NIV)

852 1 Timothy 2:8 (NIV)

853 Psalm 86:7 (NIV)

854 James 5:13 (NIV)

855 Mark 6:13 (NIV)

856 James 5:14 (NIV)

857 John 9:31 (NIV)

858 James 5:16 (NIV)

859 Revelation 4:11 (NIV)

860 Genesis 2:3 (NIV)

861 1 Peter 1:8-9 (NIV)

862 Psalm 62:1 (NIV)

863 Hebrews 1:3 (NIV)

864 Psalm 80:17 (NIV)

865 John 16:13 (NIV)

866 1 Corinthians 2:4-6 (NIV)

867 John 16:8 (NIV)

868 Job 3:26 (NIV)

869 Ephesians 4:2 (NIV)

870 Matthew 11:29 (NIV)

871 Jeremiah 31:25 (NIV)

872 Matthew 11:28 (NIV)

873 Isaiah 57:20 (NIV)

874 Proverbs 4:16 (NIV)

875 Titus 1:16 (NIV)

876 Hebrews 3:18 (NIV)

877 Philippians 4:13 (NIV)

878 2 Corinthians 12:9 (NIV)

879 Revelation 7:15 (NIV)

880 Psalm 91:1 (NIV)

881 Isaiah 45:19c (NIV)

882 Psalm 145:17 (NIV)

883 Psalm 19:8a (NIV)

884 Psalm 119:137 (NIV)

885 Luke 1:49 (NIV)

886 Psalm 71:19 (NIV)

887 Psalm 47:7 (NIV)

888 Psalm 48:10 (NIV)

889 1 Timothy 1:15 (NIV)

890 Mark 2:17 (NIV)

891 Psalm 35:23 (NIV)

892 1 John 2:1 (NIV)

893 Job 17:1 (NIV)

894 Galatians 5:5 (NIV)

895 Luke 13:18 (NIV)

896 Romans 14:17 (NIV)

897 Proverbs 30:5 (NIV)

898 Psalm 119:160 (NIV)

899 Luke 11:28 (NIV)

900 Psalm 119:172 (NIV)

901 Matthew 25:32 (NIV)

902 Matthew 13:49 (NIV)

903 Romans 6:23 (NIV)

904 Matthew 13:43 (NIV)

905 Hebrews 9:22 (NIV)

906 Psalm 66:15 (NIV)

907 1 John 3:4 (NIV)

908 Exodus 29:36a (NIV)

909 2 Kings 20:3a (NIV)

910 Genesis 22:2 (NIV)

911 Isaiah 1:11b (NIV)

912 Mark 12:33 (NIV)

913 Hebrews 10:4 (NIV)

914 Hebrews 10:10 (NIV)

915 1 John 4:8 (NIV)

916 1 John 4:10 (NIV)

917 Revelation 1:5b-6 (NIV)

918 1 Peter 2:5 (NIV)

919 1 Corinthians 6:15a (NIV)

920 Romans 12:1 (NIV)

921 Psalm 113:2 (NIV)

922 Hebrews 13:15 (NIV)

923 1 Timothy 6:18 (NIV)

924 Hebrews 13:16 (NIV)

925 Romans 1:18 (NIV)

926 1 Thessalonians 5:9 (NIV)

927 Psalm 68:20 (NIV)

928 Hebrews 2:3 (NIV)

929 James 1:18 (NIV)

930 Ephesians 1:13a (NIV)

931 John 14:6 (NIV)

932 Acts 4:12 (NIV)

933 Acts 2:21 (NIV)

934 Psalm 116:13 (NIV)

935 John 6:37 (NIV)

936 Psalm 69:13 (NIV)

937 Matthew 11:29 (NIV)

938 Psalm 62:1 (NIV)

939 John 4:14 (NIV)

[940] Isaiah 12:3 (NIV)

[941] John 8:12 (NIV)

[942] Psalm 27:1a (NIV)

[943] Matthew 13:43 (NIV)

[944] Psalm 37:39 (NIV)

[945] Acts 2:26 (NIV)

[946] Psalm 13:5 (NIV)

[947] Proverbs 16:25 (NIV)

[948] Proverbs 10:16 (NIV)

[949] Jeremiah 17:9 (NIV)

[950] 1 John 1:8 (NIV)

[951] Proverbs 26:12 (NIV)

[952] Psalm 36:2 (NIV)

[953] Hebrews 4:13 (NIV)

[954] Jeremiah 16:17 (NIV)

[955] Romans 1:20 (NIV)

[956] John 15:22 (NIV)

[957] 2 Corinthians 9:15 (NIV)

[958] Romans 6:23 (NIV)

[959] Romans 3:25a (NIV)

[960] 2 Corinthians 5:21 (NIV)

[961] John 8:36 (NIV)

[962] John 8:34 (NIV)

963 Matthew 4:1 (NIV)

964 Hebrews 4:15 (NIV)

965 Psalm 139:23 (NIV)

966 Psalm 4:4 (NIV)

967 Psalm 40:8 (NIV)

968 Psalm 119:11 (NIV)

969 Luke 22:69 (NIV)

970 1 John 2:1 (NIV)

971 Psalm 48:14 (NIV)

972 John 14:16-17 (NIV)

973 Psalm 32:8 (NIV)

974 John 14:26 (NIV)

975 John 17:17 (NIV)

976 John 16:13a (NIV)

977 1 John 3:1a (NIV)

978 Romans 8:14 (NIV)

979 Psalm 119:28 (NIV)

980 Ephesians 3:16 (NIV)

981 1 Corinthians 2:3 (NIV)

982 Romans 8:26 (NIV)

983 Isaiah 55:8 (NIV)

984 1 Corinthians 2:10b-11 (NIV)

985 John 5:31-31 (NIV)

[986] John 15:26 (NIV)

[987] John 1:12 (NIV)

[988] Romans 8:16 (NIV)

[989] Galatians 5:6 (NIV)

[990] James 2:26 (NIV)

[991] Psalm 25:9 (NIV)

[992] 1 Peter 3:4 (NIV)

[993] Hebrews 12:28-29 (NIV)

[994] 1 Thessalonians 5:19 (NIV)

[995] Psalm 115:3 (NIV)

[996] Psalm 136:26a (NIV)

[997] Deuteronomy 10:17 (NIV)

[998] Psalm 136:2 (NIV)

[999] Lamentations 3:25 (NIV)

[1000] 1 Chronicles 16:34 (NIV)

[1001] Psalm 94:11 (NIV)

[1002] Romans 1:21 (NIV)

[1003] Romans 6:23 (NIV)

[1004] 2 Corinthians 9:15 (NIV)

[1005] 1 Corinthians 15:54 (NIV)

[1006] 1 Corinthians 15:57 (NIV)

[1007] Acts 2:21 (NIV)

[1008] Psalm 118:21 (NIV)

1009 Matthew 7:13 (NIV)

1010 Psalm 118:19 (NIV)

1011 James 1:17 (NIV)

1012 Ephesians 5:19b-20 (NIV)

1013 Psalm 19:14 (NIV)

1014 Colossians 3:17 (NIV)

1015 Psalm 34:1 (NIV)

1016 1 Thessalonians 5:16-18 (NIV)

1017 Psalm 93:1 (NIV)

1018 Revelation 11:16-17 (NIV)

1019 Job 38:8-11 NIV)

1020 Genesis 1:9 NIV)

1021 Luke 17:27 (NIV))

1022 Genesis 7:18 (NIV)

1023 Genesis 24:67a (NIV)

1024 Genesis 24:14a (NIV)

1025 Hebrews 11:23 (NIV)

1026 Exodus 2:10 NIV)

1027 Hebrews 11:29 (NIV)

1028 Exodus 14:16 (NIV)

1029 Deuteronomy 31:8a (NIV)

1030 Exodus 17:6ab (NIV)

1031 Psalm 77:14 (NIV)

1032 John 2:9a (NIV)

1033 John 14:11 (NIV)

1034 John 6:19 (NIV)

1035 Colossians 1:18 (NIV)

1036 Ephesians 5:25-27 (NIV)

1037 Matthew 24:21 (NIV)

1038 Revelation 16:4 (NIV)

1039 Psalm 46:4 (NIV)

1040 Revelation 22:1-2a (NIV)

1041 Deuteronomy 4:29 (NIV)

1042 Psalm 42:1 (NIV)

1043 Psalm 89:11 (NIV)

1044 Jeremiah 10:12 (NIV)

1045 Psalm 92:5 (NIV)

1046 Job 9:4 (NIV)

1047 1 Chronicles 16:14 (NIV)

1048 Romans 11:33 (NIV)

1049 1 Corinthians 2:10b (NIV)

1050 1 Corinthians 2:13 (NIV))

1051 Proverbs 13:22 (NIV)

1052 Ecclesiastes 7:11 (NIV)

1053 Haggai 1:7 (NIV)

1054 Proverbs 14:8 (NIV)

1055 Proverbs 3:7 (NIV)

1056 Job 28:28 (NIV)

1057 Psalm 33:11 (NIV)

1058 Isaiah 28:29 (NIV)

1059 Psalm 19:14 (NIV)

1060 Psalm 49:3 (NIV)

1061 Proverbs 20:15 (NIV)

1062 Job 28:18 (NIV)

1063 Luke 6:45 (NIV)

1064 Psalm 37:30 (NIV)

1065 Matthew 7:7 (NIV)

1066 James 1:5 (NIV)

1067 John 10:30 (NIV)

1068 Hebrews 1:3a (NIV)

1069 John 1:3 (NIV)

1070 Psalm 33:6 (NIV)

1071 Matthew 5:18 (NIV)

1072 Isaiah 40:8 (NIV)

1073 Genesis 1:27 (NIV)

1074 James 1:18 (NIV)

1075 Isaiah 64:6 (NIV)

1076 1 John 1:10 (NIV)

1077 Matthew 1:23 (NIV)

1078 John 1:14 (NIV)

1079 John 3:16 (NIV)

1080 Psalm 107:20 (NIV)

1081 Jeremiah 16:17 (NIV)

1082 Psalm 119:11 (NIV)

1083 2 Timothy 3:16-17 (NIV)

1084 Proverbs 30:5 (NIV)

1085 Psalm 139:23 (NIV)

1086 Hebrews 4:12 (NIV)

1087 Romans 8:1-2 (NIV)

1088 John 5:24 (NIV)

1089 Isaiah 40:28abc (NIV)

1090 Revelation 14:7b (NIV)

1091 John 16:13a (NIV)

1092 John 4:24 (NIV)

1093 Romans 14:11 (NIV)

1094 Psalm 95:6-7 (NIV)

1095 Isaiah 47:4 (NIV)

1096 Psalm 29:2 (NIV)

1097 John 1:1 (NIV)

1098 Hebrews 1:6 (NIV)

1099 John 18:37abc (NIV)

1100 Matthew 2:1-2 (NIV)

1101 Isaiah 7:14 (NIV)

1102 Matthew 2:11a (NIV)

1103 Proverbs 16:2 (NIV)

1104 Matthew 15:9 (NIV)

1105 Job 15:20 (NIV)

1106 Revelation 14:11 (NIV)

1107 Exodus 20:4 (NIV)

1108 Revelation 22:9b (NIV)

1109 1 Peter 2:4-5 (NIV)

1110 Romans 12:1 (NIV)

1111 Romans 8:28 (NIV)

1112 Proverbs 16:6 (NIV)

1113 Job 22:15 (NIV)

1114 Proverbs 4:14 (NIV)

1115 Job 40:4 (NIV)

1116 Proverbs 30:32 (NIV)

1117 Isaiah 5:21 (NIV)

1118 Proverbs 3:7 (NIV)

1119 Matthew 18:6 (NIV)

1120 Proverbs 28:10 (NIV)

1121 Isaiah 1:17 (NIV)

1122 Proverbs 28:5 (NIV)

1123 Deuteronomy 5:32 (NIV)

[1124] Proverbs 4:27 (NIV)

[1125] Deuteronomy 30:15(NIV)

[1126] Proverbs 11:19 (NIV)

[1127] Exodus 5:2 (NIV)

[1128] Proverbs 5:22 (NIV)

[1129] John 10:31-32 (NIV)

[1130] Proverbs 17:13 (NIV)

[1131] Philippians 2:9-11 (NIV)

[1132] Proverbs 14:19 (NIV)

[1133] Hosea 14:9 (NIV)

[1134] Proverbs 12:15 (NIV)

[1135] Jeremiah 17:5 (NIV)

[1136] Proverbs 28:26 (NIV)

[1137] Ephesians 5:15-16 (NIV)

[1138] Proverbs 13:16 (NIV)

[1139] Ecclesiastes 8:5 (NIV)

[1140] Proverbs 10:8 (NIV)

[1141] Psalm 35:19 (NIV)

[1142] Proverbs 10:10 (NIV)

[1143] Job 13:5 (NIV)

[1144] Proverbs 17:28 (NIV)

[1145] James 1:19-20 (NIV)

[1146] Proverbs 29:11 (NIV)

1147 Revelation 3:19 (NIV)

1148 Proverbs 17:10 (NIV)

1149 Psalm 12:7-8 (NIV)

1150 Proverbs 26:1 (NIV)

1151 2 Timothy 2:23 (NIV)

1152 Proverbs 20:3 (NIV)

1153 Exodus 8:15 (NIV)

1154 Proverbs 26:11 (NIV)

1155 Daniel 3:19 (NIV)

1156 Proverbs 27:3 (NIV)

1157 Job 34:21 (NIV)

1158 Proverbs 15:3 (NIV)

1159 Luke 2:10 (NIV)

1160 Proverbs 15:30 (NIV)

1161 Jeremiah 23:18 (NIV)

1162 Proverbs 2:20 (NIV)

1163 Deuteronomy 29:29 (NIV)

1164 Proverbs 25:27 (NIV)

1165 Psalm 119:103 (NIV)

1166 Proverbs 24:13 (NIV)

1167 Psalm 22:22 (NIV)

1168 Proverbs 3:4 (NIV)

1169 Job 4:4 (NIV)

1170 Proverbs 15:23 (NIV)

1171 Job 28:15 (NIV)

1172 Proverbs 22:1 (NIV)

1173 Psalm 94:21 (NIV)

1174 Proverbs 18:5 (NIV)

1175 Isaiah 3:10 (NIV)

1176 Proverbs 12:14 (NIV)

1177 2 Corinthians 5:10 (NIV)

1178 Proverbs 14:14 (NIV)

1179 Romans 13:7 (NIV)

1180 Proverbs 3:27 (NIV)

1181 1 Peter 3:13 (NIV)

1182 Proverbs 12:21 (NIV)

1183 Psalm 66:18-19 (NIV)

1184 Proverbs 15:29 (NIV)

1185 James 4:4 (NIV)

1186 Proverbs 12:26 (NIV)

1187 Isaiah 10:1-2 (NIV)

1188 Proverbs 29:7 (NIV)

1189 Colossians 3:9-10 (NIV)

1190 Proverbs 13:5 (NIV)

1191 Matthew 22:13 (NIV)

1192 Proverbs 13:9 (NIV)

1193 Job 18:17 (NIV)

1194 Proverbs 10:7 (NIV)

1195 Revelation 7:16a (NIV)

1196 Proverbs 10:3 (NIV)

1197 1 Peter 3:15ab (NIV)

1198 Proverbs 15:28 (NIV)

1199 1 John 3:13 (NIV)

1200 Proverbs 29:27 (NIV)

1201 2 Corinthians 10:4 (NIV)

1202 Proverbs 12:12 (NIV)

1203 Leviticus 26:17 (NIV)

1204 Proverbs 28:1 (NIV)

1205 James 3:9 (NIV)

1206 Proverbs 15:4 (NIV)

1207 Nehemiah 2:1b-2 (NIV)

1208 Proverbs 15:13 (NIV)

1209 Isaiah 2:11 (NIV)

1210 Proverbs 16:18 (NIV)

1211 1 Samuel 2:7 (NIV)

1212 Proverbs 16:19 (NIV)

1213 Ezekiel 37:11 (NIV)

1214 Proverbs 17:22 (NIV)

1215 Psalm 109:22 (NIV)

1216 Proverbs 18:14 (NIV)

1217 2 Samuel 22:29 (NIV)

1218 Proverbs 20:27 (NIV)

1219 Matthew 23:12 (NIV)

1220 Proverbs 29:23 (NIV)

1221 1 Thessalonians 4:3-5 (NIV)

1222 Proverbs 2:18 (NIV)

1223 John 1:6 (NIV)

1224 Proverbs 25:13 (NIV)

1225 2 Corinthians 1:12 (NIV)

1226 Proverbs 2:7 (NIV)

1227 Psalm 37:29 (NIV)

1228 Proverbs 2:21 (NIV)

1229 John 7:17 (NIV)

1230 Proverbs 3:32 (NIV)

1231 Job 4:6 (NIV)

1232 Proverbs 11:3 (NIV)

1233 Romans 10:10 (NIV)

1234 Proverbs 12:6 (NIV)

1235 Matthew 18:21-22 (NIV)

1236 Proverbs 14:9 (NIV)

1237 2 Corinthians 5:1 (NIV)

1238 Proverbs 14:11 (NIV)

1239 1 Peter 3:12 (NIV)

1240 Proverbs 15:8 (NIV)

1241 Psalm 37:27 (NIV)

1242 Proverbs 16:17 (NIV)

1243 Acts 7:59 (NIV)

1244 Proverbs 29:10 (NIV)

1245 Ester 3:6 (NIV)

1246 Proverbs 14:2 (NIV)

1247 2 Peter 1:4 (NIV)

1248 Proverbs 11:6 (NIV)

1249 John 1:3 (NIV)

1250 Proverbs 3:19 (NIV)

1251 Job 28:15 (NIV)

1252 Proverbs 3:13 (NIV)

1253 Job 22:22 (NIV)

1254 Proverbs 2:6 (NIV)

1255 Matthew 4:4 (NIV)

1256 Proverbs 4:5 (NIV)

1257 Psalm 1:1-2 (NIV)

1258 Proverbs 10:23 (NIV)

1259 Luke 11:27 (NIV)

1260 Proverbs 8:1 (NIV)

1261 Matthew 13:44 (NIV)

[1262] Proverbs 4:7 (NIV)

[1263] Jeremiah 6:29:11 (NIV)

[1264] Proverbs 19:8 (NIV)

[1265] Exodus 18:24-26a (NIV)

[1266] Proverbs 3:21 (NIV)

[1267] 1 Corinthians 3:9 (NIV)

[1268] Proverbs 24:3 (NIV)

[1269] Ecclesiastes 12:13 (NIV))

[1270] Proverbs 9:10 (NIV)

[1271] Psalm 1:1a NIV)

[1272] Proverbs 4:14 (NIV)

[1273] Psalm 1:1b (NIV)

[1274] Proverbs 14:12 (NIV)

[1275] Psalm 1:1c (NIV)

[1276] Job 17:2 (NIV)

[1277] Psalm 1:2a (NIV)

[1278] Romans 7:22 (NIV)

[1279] Psalm 1:2b (NIV)

[1280] Psalm 119:97 (NIV)

[1281] Psalm 1:3a (NIV)

[1282] Jeremiah 17:8a (NIV)

[1283] Psalm 1:3b (NIV)

[1284] Psalm 37:19 NIV)

1285 Psalm 1:3c (NIV)

1286 Jeremiah 29:11 (NIV)

1287 Psalm 1:4ab (NIV)

1288 Psalm 11:6 (NIV)

1289 Psalm 1:5a (NIV)

1290 2 Corinthians 5:10 (NIV)

1291 Psalm1:5b (NIV)

1292 Luke 16:23 (NIV)

1293 Psalm 1:6a (NIV)

1294 Psalm 5:12 (NIV)

1295 Psalm 1:6b (NIV)

1296 Psalm 37:38 (NIV)

1297 Psalm 8:1a (NIV)

1298 Philippians 2:9-10 (NIV)

1299 Psalm 8:1b (NIV)

1300 Hebrews 4:14 (NIV)

1301 Psalm 8:2 (NIV)

1302 Matthew 21:16 (NIV)

1303 Psalm 8:3 (NIV)

1304 Isaiah 40:28 (NIV)

1305 Psalm 8:4 (NIV)

1306 John 3:16 (NIV)

1307 Psalm 8:5 (NIV)

1308 Genesis 1:27 (NIV)

1309 Psalm 8:6 (NIV)

1310 Genesis 1:28a (NIV)

1311 Psalm 8:7 (NIV)

1312 Psalm 8:8 (NIV)

1313 Genesis 1:26 (NIV)

1314 Psalm 8:9 (NIV)

1315 Jude 1:24-25 (NIV)

1316 Psalm 14:1a (NIV)

1317 2 Corinthians 4:4 (NIV)

1318 Psalm 14:1b (NIV)

1319 John 3:19 (NIV)

1320 Psalm 14:2a (NIV)

1321 John 17:1 (NIV)

1322 Psalm 14:2b (NIV)

1323 1 John 5:20a (NIV)

1324 Psalm 14:2c (NIV)

1325 Luke 19:10 (NIV)

1326 Psalm 14:3a (NIV)

1327 Romans 5:8 (NIV)

1328 Psalm 14:3b (NIV)

1329 2 Corinthians 5:21 (NIV)

1330 Psalm 14:4a (NIV)

1331 Mark 10:1 (NIV)

1332 Psalm 14:4b (NIV)

1333 Acts 2:21 (NIV

1334 Psalm 14:5a (NIV)

1335 Romans 8:1 (NIV)

1336 Psalm 14:5b (NIV)

1337 Matthew 9:10 (NIV)

1338 Psalm 14:6a (NIV)

1339 James 5:20 (NIV)

1340 Psalm 14:6b (NIV)

1341 Matthew 11:28 (NIV)

1342 Psalm 14:7a (NIV)

1343 Acts 13:23 (NIV)

1344 Psalm 14:7b (NIV)

1345 1 Peter 5:10 (NIV)

1346 Psalm 15:1a (NIV)

1347 Ephesians 3:16-17a (NIV)

1348 Psalm 15:1b (NIV)

1349 John 4:21 (NIV)

1350 Psalm 15:2a (NIV)

1351 Ephesians 1:4a (NIV)

1352 Psalm 15:2b (NIV)

1353 Romans 3:22a (NIV)

[1354] Psalm 15:2c (NIV)

[1355] 1 Peter 1:22 (NIV)

[1356] Psalm 15:3a (NIV)

[1357] James 1:26 (NIV)

[1358] Psalm 15:3b (NIV)

[1359] Romans 15:2 (NIV)

[1360] Psalm 15:3c (NIV)

[1361] James 4:11a (NIV)

[1362] Psalm 15:4a (NIV)

[1363] Romans 12:9b (NIV)

[1364] Psalm 15:4b (NIV)

[1365] 1 John 3:16 (NIV)

[1366] Psalm 15:4c (NIV)

[1367] Colossians 3:9-10 (NIV)

[1368] Psalm 15:4d (NIV)

[1369] James 5:12 (NIV)

[1370] Psalm 15:5a (NIV)

[1371] Luke 11:41 (NIV)

[1372] Psalm 15:5b (NIV)

[1373] Titus 2:12 (NIV)

[1374] Psalm 15:5c (NIV)

[1375] 1 Corinthians 15:58 (NIV)

[1376] Psalm 19:1 (NIV)

1377 Isaiah 40:26ab (NIV)

1378 Psalm 19:2 (NIV)

1379 1 Corinthians 1:5 (NIV)

1380 Psalm 19:3-4a (NIV)

1381 Romans 1:20 (NIV)

1382 Psalm 19:4b (NIV)

1383 Isaiah 40:22b (NIV)

1384 Psalm 19:5-6 (NIV)

1385 Proverbs 4:18 (NIV)

1386 Psalm 19:7-8a (NIV)

1387 John 8:47a (NIV)

1388 Psalm 19:8b (NIV)

1389 1 John 2:8 (NIV)

1390 Psalm 19:9a (NIV)

1391 Isaiah 33:6 (NIV)

1392 Psalm 19:9b-10a (NIV)

1393 Psalm 12:6 (NIV)

1394 Psalm 19:10b (NIV)

1395 Psalm 119:103 (NIV)

1396 Psalm 19:11 (NIV)

1397 John 3:36 (NIV)

1398 Psalm 19:12 (NIV)

1399 Matthew 7:3-4 (NIV)

[1400] Psalm 19:13 (NIV)

[1401] Psalm 119:11 (NIV)

[1402] Psalm 19:14a (NIV)

[1403] Romans 12:1 (NIV)

[1404] Psalm 19:14b (NIV)

[1405] Job 19:25 (NIV)

[1406] Psalm 23:1a (NIV)

[1407] Hebrews 13:20-21 (NIV)

[1408] Psalm 23:1b (NIV)

[1409] Philippians 4:19 (NIV)

[1410] Psalm 23:2a (NIV)

[1411] John 10:9 (NIV)

[1412] Psalm 23:2b (NIV)

[1413] Matthew 11:28 (NIV)

[1414] Psalm 23:3a (NIV)

[1415] 1 Thessalonians 5:23 (NIV)

[1416] Psalm 23:3b (NIV)

[1417] Acts 2:28 (NIV)

[1418] Psalm 23:4a (NIV)

[1419] Matthew 26:38 (NIV)

[1420] Psalm 23:4b (NIV)

[1421] Matthew 14:27 (NIV)

[1422] Psalm 23:4c (NIV)

1423 Matthew 28:20b (NIV)

1424 Psalm 23:4d (NIV)

1425 2 Corinthians 1:3-4 (NIV)

1426 Psalm 23:5a (NIV)

1427 John 14:27ab (NIV)

1428 Psalm 23:5b (NIV)

1429 1 Peter 2:5 (NIV)

1430 Psalm 23:5c (NIV)

1431 Romans 5:15 (NIV)

1432 Psalm 23:6a (NIV)

1433 Philippians 1:6 (NIV)

1434 Psalm 23:6b (NIV)

1435 Philippians 3:20 (NIV)

1436 Psalm 24:1 (NIV)

1437 Ephesians 1:8b-10 (NIV)

1438 Psalm 24:2 (NIV)

1439 2 Peter 3:5 (NIV)

1440 Psalm 24:3 (NIV)

1441 Colossians 3:1 (NIV)

1442 Psalm 24:4 (NIV)

1443 Romans 10:10 (NIV)

1444 Psalm 24:5 (NIV)

1445 Ephesians 1:3 (NIV)

[1446] Psalm 24:6 (NIV)

[1447] Matthew 7:7 (NIV)

[1448] Psalm 24:7 (NIV)

[1449] John 10:9 (NIV)

[1450] Psalm 24:8 (NIV)

[1451] Revelation 19:11 (NIV)

[1452] Psalm 24:9 (NIV)

[1453] Revelation 3:20 (NIV)

[1454] Psalm 24:10 (NIV)

[1455] Mark 8:29 (NIV)

[1456] Psalm 46:1 (NIV)

[1457] John 16:33 (NIV)

[1458] Psalm 46:2 (NIV)

[1459] Revelation 16:20 (NIV)

[1460] Psalm 46:3 (NIV)

[1461] Revelation 8:8a (NIV)

[1462] Psalm 46:4 (NIV)

[1463] Revelation 22:1-2a (NIV)

[1464] Psalm 46:5 (NIV)

[1465] Revelation 22:3 (NIV)

[1466] Psalm 46:6 (NIV)

[1467] Revelation 19:15 (NIV)

[1468] Psalm 46:7 (NIV)

1469 Revelation 19:14 (NIV)

1470 Psalm 46:8 (NIV)

1471 Revelation 19:21 (NIV)

1472 Psalm 46:9 (NIV)

1473 Isaiah 2:4 (NIV)

1474 Psalm 46:10 (NIV)

1475 Philippians 2:9-10 (NIV)

1476 Psalm 46:11 (NIV)

1477 Ephesians 2:6 (NIV)

1478 Psalm 84:1 (NIV)

1479 Matthew 8:20 (NIV)

1480 Psalm 84:2 (NIV)

1481 Matthew 7:8 (NIV)

1482 Psalm 84:3 (NIV)

1483 Matthew 10:29 (NIV)

1484 Psalm 84:4 (NIV)

1485 Luke 17:15 (NIV)

1486 Psalm 84:5 (NIV)

1487 Matthew 11:6 (NIV)

1488 Psalm 84:6 (NIV)

1489 Revelation 21:6 (NIV)

1490 Psalm 84:7 (NIV)

1491 2 Corinthians 5:10 (NIV)

[1492] Psalm 84:8 (NIV)

[1493] Matthew 17:5 (NIV)

[1494] Psalm 84:9 (NIV)

[1495] Acts 10:37-38 (NIV)

[1496] Psalm 84:10 (NIV)

[1497] 2 Peter 3:8 (NIV)

[1498] Psalm 84:11 (NIV)

[1499] Matthew 7:11 (NIV)

[1500] Psalm 84:12 (NIV)

[1501] Romans 15:13 (NIV)

[1502] Psalm 95:1 (NIV)

[1503] 1 Chronicles 16:23 (NIV)

[1504] Psalm 95:2 (NIV)

[1505] Ephesians 5:19b-20 (NIV)

[1506] Psalm 95:3 (NIV)

[1507] John 18:37abc (NIV)

[1508] Psalm 95:4 (NIV)

[1509] Psalm 135:6 (NIV)

[1510] Psalm 95:5 (NIV)

[1511] John 1:3 (NIV)

[1512] Psalm 95:6 (NIV)

[1513] Philippians 2:9-10 (NIV)

[1514] Psalm 95:7a (NIV)

1515 John 10:9 (NIV)

1516 Psalm 95:7b (NIV)

1517 Mark 9:7 (NIV)

1518 Psalm 95:8 (NIV)

1519 Ephesians 4:18 (NIV)

1520 Psalm 95:9 (NIV)

1521 1 Corinthians 10:9 (NIV)

1522 Psalm 95:10 (NIV)

1523 Hebrews 3:17 (NIV)

1524 Psalm 95:11 (NIV)

1525 Hebrews 4:1 (NIV)

1526 Psalm 138:1 (NIV)

1527 1 Corinthians 8:5-6 (NIV)

1528 Psalm 138:2a (NIV)

1529 Matthew 12:6 (NIV)

1530 Psalm 138:2b (NIV)

1531 2 Corinthians 1:20 (NIV)

1532 Psalm 138:3 (NIV)

1533 Isaiah 58:9a (NIV)

1534 Psalm 138:4 (NIV)

1535 Revelation 1:4b-5a (NIV)

1536 Psalm 138:5 (NIV)

12 Isaiah 6:3 (NIV)

1538 Psalm 138:6 (NIV)

1539 Isaiah 57:15 (NIV)

1540 Psalm 138:7a (NIV)

1541 Psalm 9:9 (NIV)

1542 Psalm 138:7b (NIV)

1543 Isaiah 41:10 (NIV)

1544 Psalm 138:8 (NIV)

1545 Philippians 1:6 (NIV)

1546 Psalm 139:1-2 (NIV)

1547 Matthew 10:30 (NIV)

1548 Psalm 139:3-4 (NIV)

1549 Hebrews 4:13 (NIV)

1550 Psalm 139:5-6 (NIV)

1551 Acts 2:25 (NIV)

1552 Psalm 139:7-8 (NIV)

1553 Matthew 28:20b (NIV)

1554 Psalm 139:9-10 (NIV)

1555 John 10:28 (NIV)

1556 Psalm 139:11-12 (NIV)

1557 1 John 1:5b (NIV)

1558 Psalm 139:13-14 (NIV)

1559 James 1:18 (NIV)

1560 Psalm 139:15-16 (NIV)

1561 Ephesians 1:3-4a (NIV)

1562 Psalm 139:17-18 (NIV)

1563 Romans 11:33-34a (NIV)

1564 Psalm 139:19-20 (NIV)

1565 2 Peter 3:9 (NIV)

1566 Psalm 139:21-22 (NIV)

1567 Philippians 3:18 (NIV)

1568 Psalm 139:23-24 (NIV)

1569 1 Thessalonians 2:4b (NIV)

1570 Psalm 150:1ab (NIV)

1571 Hebrews 6:19-20a (NIV)

1572 Psalm 150:1c (NIV)

1573 Hebrews 9:24 (NIV)

1574 Psalm 150:2a (NIV)

1575 Mark 5:29-31 (NIV)

1576 Psalm 150:2b (NIV)

1577 Deuteronomy 32:3 (NIV)

1578 Psalm 150:3a (NIV)

1579 Psalm 47:5 (NIV)

1580 Psalm 150:3b (NIV)

1581 Revelation 14:2 (NIV)

1582 Psalm 150:4a (NIV)

1583 Exodus 15:20-21a (NIV)

1584 Psalm 150:4b (NIV)

1585 Psalm 33:3 (NIV)

1586 Psalm 150:5a (NIV)

1587 2 Chronicles 5:13ab (NIV)

1588 Psalm 150:5b (NIV)

1589 Nehemiah 12:27 (NIV)

1590 Psalm 150:6 (NIV)

1591 Psalm 145:21 (NIV)

Printed in the USA
CPSIA information can be obtained
at www.ICGtesting.com
LVHW081547240624
783873LV00016B/1321

9 781456 637149